The Melville Boys

The Melville Boys

by
Norm Foster

Playwrights Canada Press
Toronto•Canada

The Melville Boys © Copyright 1984 Norm Foster

Playwrights Canada Press
54 Wolseley Street, 2nd Floor
Toronto, Ontario CANADA M5T 1A5
(416) 703-0201   fax (416) 703-0059
info@puc.ca   http://www.puc.ca

Playwrights Canada Press acknowledges the support of
The Canada Council for the Arts for our publishing programme and
the Ontario Arts Council.

Cover design by Lisa Dimson. Cover photo by Don Johnson.

Canadian Cataloguing in Publication Data

Foster, Norm, 1949-
    The Melville boys

A play.
ISBN 0-88754-452-5

I. Title
PS8561.0865M44 1986   C812'.54   C86-093338-5
PR9199.2.F679M44 1986

First edition: May 8, 1986. Second printing: August 1987. Third printing: August 1989.
Fourth printing: May 1992. Fifth printing: September 1994. Sixth printing: May 1999.
Nineth printing: October 2002. Seventh printing: September 2000. Eighth printing: July 2001.

Printed and bound by AGMV Printing, Longueill, Québec, Canada.

The Melville Boys was first produced by Theatre New Brunswick, Fredericton, in October 1984, with the following cast:

OWEN Melville	Robert King
LEE Melville	John Dolan
MARY	Deborah Kimmett
LORETTA	Patricia Vanstone

Directed by Malcolm Black
Set and Costumes Designed by Patrick Clark
Lighting Designed by David Gibbons

CHARACTERS

LEE Melville	Mid-thirties. Working class.
OWEN Melville	Late twenties. Working class. Almost child-like in his outlook. Both Lee and Owen smoke throughout the action.
MARY	Early thirties. A smart woman but not completely sure of herself.
LORETTA	Mid-twenties. Blonde. Equally as smart as her sister, but she chooses to throw herself into life more.

Blonds have more fun....

THE SCENE

Present day. Mid-September. A cabin belonging to the uncle of Lee and Owen Melville. The entrance to the cabin is upstage and slightly to the right of centre. Left of the entrance, and coming out from the back wall at ninety degrees, is a counter which divides the back of the room. Left of the counter is the kitchen area. There are cupboards and a sink against the back wall. Left of the sink is an old refrigerator. Beside the refrigerator is a small trash can. Against the wall left is an old stove, on which sits a coffee pot. Downstage from the stove is a small set of bookshelves and, above the shelves, a window which looks out onto an enclosed porch. Downstage from the shelves is the screen door which leads into the porch and, beyond that, another door which leads out of the porch and down to the lake. Downstage from the kitchen area is a table and four chairs. Downstage right is an old couch and, beside the couch, left, a small end table. There are a couple of magazines on the end table. To the right of the couch is an old rocking chair and, beside the rocking chair, another small table. Against the wall right is a tall lamp. Upstage from the lamp is the exit to the bedroom. The door opens into the bedroom. Upstage from the bedroom door is a wood stove and, behind the wood stove, the wall angles in for a couple of feet and then turns upstage again. Set against this wall is the bathroom door. Upstage right on the back wall is a row of coat hooks. On one of the hooks hangs a sweater coat belonging to Aunt Rose. On the wall right hangs a deer head and, over the door, downstage left, a mounted fish. On the shelves is a box of Kleenex. There is a note on the kitchen table.

ACT ONE

SCENE 1

> OWEN *enters upstage centre. He is carrying a tackle box and a rifle. He is dressed for a weekend at the lake, and he also wears a straw cowboy hat.*

OWEN (*raising his hands in an open arms type of greeting*) Hello country life you son of a bitch!

LEE (*offstage*) Owen?

OWEN What?

LEE (*offstage*) Can you give me a hand with this stuff?

OWEN Yeah, be right there! (*sets the tackle box on the counter, and begins to speak to himself as if he is narrating a story*) And so, Jesse and Frank had outrun the posse once again. They'd be safe here... (*moves downstage quickly and hides behind the couch; pokes his head up*) for the time bein'. (*moves slowly right, still crouched down*) No, it wasn't an easy life stayin' one step ahead of the law. Never knowing what danger lay behind the next bedroom door. (*throws open the bedroom door and points the rifle inside, making shooting sounds with his mouth; stops, still staring into the bedroom*) Oh, sorry, folks. My mistake. (*moves downstage in front of the couch*) Yep, an ordinary man woulda cracked under this kinda pressure. But, these weren't no ordinary men. No sir. These were the James boys. Jesse, the young one... cool and calm, with a certain boyish charm. (*runs his hands through his hair to emphasize charm*) And Frank, the older brother...

LEE (*offstage*) Owen!

OWEN The obnoxious one. (*notices the deer head on the wall right; tips his hat*) Mornin' ma'am. (*moves left towards the screen door*) Jesse may have been mean, but he always had a kind word for a pretty gal. (*exits*)

LEE enters upstage centre. He is carrying two fishing rods, a tackle box, a bag of groceries, a suitcase, and he has a pair of binoculars around his neck.

LEE   Damn it, Owen, what the hell are you doing in here? (*moves around to the kitchen area and looks around*) Owen?!

When there is no answer, LEE struggles to put the bag of groceries on the counter. The tackle box and suitcase fall to the floor.

LEE   I'll strangle him. Owen!

OWEN   (*enters upstage centre*) Yeah?

LEE   Where the hell have you been?

OWEN   (*with his best John Wayne voice*) I've been out checkin' the grounds, cap'n.

LEE   Well, would you give me a hand, please?

OWEN   You brought all this stuff in by yourself? (*picks up the suitcase*)

LEE   Yes, I did, thank you.

OWEN   You should've made two trips. (*moves downstage centre*)

LEE puts the fishing rods beside the stove, and the binoculars on the shelves left.

So, what do you think of the place? Hasn't changed much in ten years, has it? I figured Aunt Rose and Uncle Will would've done some work on it. You know, fixed it up a bit. Course, Uncle Will never was one for doing any work on his vacation time. Never knew a man as lazy as that one. Here.

OWEN hands the suitcase to LEE. LEE, exasperated, takes the suitcase into the bedroom right. OWEN moves upstage to the counter and takes a six-pack out of the grocery bag.

OWEN	It's perfect for us though, don't you think? Nobody to bother us. And we've got two whole days with nothing to do but fish. You know, Lee, I don't know why we waited so long to come back here. When we were kids, we were up here every weekend. Remember? (*moves to put the beer in the refrigerator*)
LEE	(*entering from the bedroom*) Yeah, I remember.

OWEN opens up the fridge, lets out a yell, and points his gun inside the refrigerator.

What's the matter?

OWEN	I think those are the same wieners that were here the last time we were here. Yeah, I recognize the one in the middle. (*shoots the wieners, making the shooting sound with his mouth again*)
LEE	Owen, there are still three bags of groceries out in the car.
OWEN	(*closing the refrigerator*) Well, don't forget those. Those are our supplies for the weekend.
LEE	(*controlling his exasperation*) Right. Well, I guess I'd better get them then. (*exits upstage centre*)
OWEN	(*moves downstage to the table and picks up the note*) Hey, Lee! Aunt Rose left us a note! (*reads it to himself*) "Dear boys, wipe your feet." (*wipes his feet where he stands*) "You can use the boat, but make sure you wear your life jackets. And don't be reckless. And please don't leave the cabin in a mess. Take your garbage to the dump, and make sure the stove's out before you go. And don't leave any dirty dishes. Have fun. Love, Aunt Rose."

LEE enters upstage centre with the three bags of groceries.

OWEN	Wipe your feet.
LEE	What?

OWEN   Orders from Aunt Rose. We have to wipe our feet, do our dishes, and go to the dump.

LEE   Gee, I can't wait to get started.

            OWEN moves to the screen door.

            Are you going to carry that thing around with you all day?

OWEN   What, this? (*holds up the gun*) Well, I thought I might shoot some rabbit while you get things squared away here.

LEE   Rabbits aren't in season. (*moves right to hang his coat*)

OWEN   Yeah, won't they be surprised. (*laughs and looks out the screen door*) Boy, I can't wait to hit that lake. I can hear those fish now, just begging me to come and yank them out of that cold water. (*yells out the door*) It won't be long now, fishes! We'll be right down! Tell your friends! (*moves right to LEE*) Hey, you know what we should do, Lee? We should take the whole damn week off. Yeah, just phone the plant and tell them the Melville boys won't be in this week. How does that sound?

LEE   No, I don't think so. (*begins to put the groceries away*)

OWEN   Come on. Let's do it. Can't you see the look on Harvey's face when you phone him?

LEE   When I phone him? What do you mean, when I phone him?

OWEN   Well, you're the foreman. It'll sound better coming from you.

LEE   No. Forget it.

OWEN   Aw, come on.

LEE   I can't. (*moves left and puts the tackle box with the rods*)

OWEN	Sure you can.
LEE	No, the doctor says I have to start that treatment on Monday. (*moves back to the groceries*)
OWEN	I'll bet being up here for a week would do you just as much good as that treatment. More, I'll bet.
LEE	You're probably right. But, he thinks I should try it anyway. (*gives a little laugh*) Did I tell you what he said to me yesterday? I mean, this guy doesn't pull any punches...
OWEN	I wanna go fishing. (*moves left to pick up his rod and tackle box*)
LEE	What?
OWEN	I wanna go fishing. That's what we came up here for isn't it? To go fishing? So let's go.
LEE	We can't go yet.
OWEN	Why not?
LEE	Because I've got all this stuff to put away. And besides, I haven't had my breakfast yet.
OWEN	Breakfast? You haven't got time for breakfast. The fish are waiting.
LEE	They'll have to wait. I can't fish on an empty stomach.
OWEN	So, we'll take some beer out in the boat.
LEE	I don't want beer. I want food.
OWEN	Oh, Jeezus, Lee. Come on.
LEE	I'm sorry. I'm not going anywhere until I have breakfast.

OWEN   (*putting his gear back*) All right, fine! But, we're going
            to miss the best fishing. You know that. It's eleven
            o'clock already, and by the time you have your
            breakfast it'll be noon, and then I suppose you'll
            want your lunch!

LEE   You can whine all you want, Owen. It's not going to
            change my mind.

OWEN   Okay. Okay. I'll tell you this much though. Those
            fish are gonna be pissed off.

            *OWEN moves to the couch and sits. He begins
            flipping through one of the magazines on the small
            end table. LEE pulls an endless string of beer and
            junk food out of the grocery bags.*

LEE   Owen, where's the food?

OWEN   What food?

LEE   The food. The stuff we're going to eat for the next
            two days. You said you were going to stock up.

OWEN   I did stock up.

LEE   With what? All I see is beer and potato chips and
            donuts.

OWEN   Yeah.

LEE   So, where's the food? These are snacks, Owen.
            Snacks!

OWEN   (*getting up and moving to the table*) There's more.

LEE   Where?

OWEN   It's here.

LEE   So, show me. I don't see it.

OWEN   All right. Don't get excited. Do you think I'd come
            up here with no food?

OWEN pulls a loaf of bread out of one of the bags and hands it to LEE.

Give me some credit, will ya? (*reaches back into the bag and, singing some sort of fanfare, pulls out a huge jar of peanut butter*) Bon appetite. (*pronounces it as English*)

LEE   (*taking the jar, incredulously*) A jar of peanut butter?

OWEN   Yeah.

LEE   You brought one jar of peanut butter?

OWEN   Well, it's a big one.

LEE   One jar of peanut butter for the whole weekend?

OWEN   Well, how many jars of peanut butter do you want?

LEE   I want more than peanut butter! What about breakfast? I want some eggs... bacon.

OWEN   Well, you didn't tell me you wanted all that.

LEE   All what? Bacon and eggs. Is that so much?

OWEN   Well, I didn't think you were going to sit around and eat all day.

LEE   I'm not going to sit around and eat all day. I just want one good meal. Maybe two in the next forty-eight hours.

OWEN   All right, all right. I'll go to that little corner store up the road and get you some eggs. Okay?

LEE   Thank you.

OWEN   Don't mention it.

LEE   And some bacon too.

OWEN   And some bacon. (*moves left to the screen*)

LEE   And some ham.

OWEN   And some ham, sure. I'll spend the whole day up there, okay? I'll shop 'til I drop. (*waves out the door*) Hi there!

LEE   What?

OWEN   There's a couple of people out there in a boat and they're waving at me. (*opens the screen door and moves into the porch*) Yeah, hello! (*stops waving suddenly*) Oh, wait a minute now. Wait just a minute.

LEE   What's the matter?

OWEN   (*rushing back to get the binoculars*) Oh my god! (*rushes back into the porch*)

LEE   What is it? Are they in trouble?

OWEN   No, I think it's two girls!

LEE   So what?

OWEN   So what? So, if it's two girls we're two guys, that's what! (*looking out through the binoculars*) Oh, yeah. Ooh, yeah. It's two girls all right. And it's kind of hard to tell from here, but I think they're filled with lust. (*yelling out again*) Hi girls! Come on up!

LEE   Don't do that!

OWEN   Why not?

LEE   Because I don't want any women up here.

OWEN   Sure you do. This is what I brought you up here for. To have fun.

LEE   I don't want to have fun. I'm married.

OWEN   Well, I'm not. Not yet.

LEE   No, but you will be in three weeks.

OWEN	All the more reason to get them up here in a hurry. Hey! Come on up!
LEE	Owen, get away from the door!
OWEN	(*coming back inside*) You mean you really don't want a girl?
LEE	No, I don't.
OWEN	Okay. (*moving back into the porch*) Sorry girls! Only one of you can come up!!
LEE	(*rushing into the porch and pulling OWEN back*) Get away from there! What are you, crazy?
OWEN	Oh, Lee, we've gotta stay up here for the whole week now. We've gotta. I mean, look, we've got fish and women!
LEE	I told you, I can't.
OWEN	You can so.
LEE	No! I told the doctor I'd be there Monday, and I'm gonna be there.
OWEN	(*cutting him off angrily*) I can't believe this. We've got a lake filled with fish, boats filled with women, and you want to go back.
LEE	That's right.
OWEN	Okay, listen. At least do this much for me. Ask Harvey to give me the week off. I'll stay here by myself, and you can come back up next weekend and get me.
LEE	Forget it. Harvey wouldn't give it to you .
OWEN	He would if *you* asked him for me.
LEE	Well, I'm not asking.

OWEN   Oh, come on.

LEE   No.

OWEN   Goddamn it, Lee. (*moves downstage to the couch*)
What's the use of you being foreman if you won't
even pull a few strings for your own brother? You're
not going to earn my respect that way, I can tell you
that. (*sits on the couch*)

LEE   (*moving downstage to the couch*) Owen, do you really
like working there? I mean, you're always asking for
time off.

OWEN   It's all right.

LEE   (*moves right and sits on the arm of the couch*) Have you
ever thought of doing something else?

OWEN   Like what?

LEE   I don't know. You could go back to school. Learn
yourself a trade.

OWEN   I'm not going back to no school. I didn't like it when
I was there the first time.

LEE   Why not? You were doing all right. You got good
marks.

OWEN   So did you, and you quit.

LEE   I had to quit. We needed the money.

OWEN   Yeah, well, I need money now too. I mean, I am
getting married in three weeks.

LEE   So, go to night school.

OWEN   Oh, good. Night school. And when am I supposed to
see Patty? I mean, I'd say "I do" at the wedding, and
then I never would.

LEE   I just think you could be doing something better, that's all.

OWEN   So, what's better than the plant? Dad worked there. It was good enough for him. You work there. Hell, Lee, we got it made. In five years, you and me will be running that place. As it is now, they'd be lost without us.

LEE   Don't kid yourself, Owen. They could get somebody in off the street today to do what we do.

OWEN   You don't know what you're talking about. (*gets up from the couch and moves towards the door upstage centre*) I'm going to the store.

LEE   Owen, wait. (*moves left*) I was going to tell you this before, but then I figured maybe it was better to tell you after it was all decided.... Uh, after next month, I'm not going to be foreman there anymore.

OWEN   What's that supposed to mean, you're not going to be foreman anymore? They're not moving you up to the office, are they? You'd be lousy at office work. You'd go crazy there.

LEE   No, I'm not moving up. I gave Harvey my notice. I'm going to stay on for a month to help them get a new foreman worked in, and then I'm done. I'm going to take a little vacation.

OWEN   You're kidding, aren't you?

LEE   No. I've got some money saved up, so I thought I'd treat the family to a trip somewhere. I think the kids would like to see Disneyland.

OWEN   You wouldn't quit the plant. You've been there almost fifteen years. You wouldn't know what to do with yourself if you didn't go into work every day.

LEE   Look, will you stop acting as if you don't know what's going on here?

OWEN   Oh, I know what's going on all right. Yeah, you listen to one doctor... one doctor, who spends his whole day sticking a stethoscope up God knows what, and the next thing you know, you're giving up the only job you ever had in your entire life, and you're driving off to Disneyland! Is that what this doctor told you to do? Go to Disneyland?

LEE   Owen...

OWEN   Well, let me tell you something about this doctor of yours. You know, he's the same doctor who told Kenny Wilson that if he didn't stop smoking and lose some weight, he'd be dead inside a year. And you know what? Kenny still smokes, he's still fat, and he's still alive.

LEE   (*sitting on the couch*) Owen, this isn't a weight problem.

OWEN   (*sitting on the couch beside LEE*) No, the point is, he's still alive. And you know how long it's been? Huh? Almost a year and a half. So much for your doctor.

LEE   I don't care about Kenny Wilson. I've given this a lot of thought, and things being the way they are...

OWEN   Things are fine! Things are just fine. Now, on Monday morning we'll go in and we'll get your job back.

LEE   No, we won't.

OWEN   We'll tell Harvey you were just joking around. He'll understand. (*laughs*) I mean, hell, we've played enough jokes on Harvey all these years. He won't mind one more. (*gets up from the couch*) Yeah, that's what we'll do. First thing Monday morning.

LEE   Owen, will you listen to me?

OWEN   I'm going to the store.

LEE	What do you mean, you're going to the store? I'm talking to you here.

OWEN	We've got all weekend to talk. The sooner you get your breakfast, the sooner we can get out in that boat. Those fish aren't going to wait forever you know.

LEE	Owen

> *OWEN picks a bag of Cheesies off the counter and tosses them to LEE.*

OWEN	Here. This'll hold you until I get back. (*exits upstage centre*)

LEE	Owen! (*looks at the bag of Cheesies, then moves downstage in front of the couch towards the wall right*) He expects me to eat this junk? (*opens the bag reluctantly, and pops a couple into his mouth; looks up at the deer head*) Well, what are you looking at?! I'm hungry, all right?

> *Lights down.*

SCENE 2

> *A few minutes later, in the cabin. The lights come up and there is no one onstage. MARY enters the porch from offstage left. She is wearing a life jacket, and the casual clothing one might wear while boating.*

MARY	Hello? Anybody home? (*moves through the screen door left and into the living room*) Will?... Rose?

LEE	(*from the bathroom*) Hello?

MARY	Hello.

LEE	Who's there?

MARY	It's Mary.

LEE   Just a minute.

MARY   (*friendly*) Hey, since when do you two come up here without stopping in to say hello? (*picks up the bag of Cheesies which is now sitting on the table*) What's the matter? You too good for us country folk all of a sudden? Next time you do that you'll get a good swift kick in the rear. (*puts some Cheesies in her mouth*)

      LEE enters from the bathroom carrying a newspaper.

      Oh... uh... excuse me. I... I was out in the boat there, and I saw somebody waving. I thought it was Will, so I came up.

LEE   (*moving downstage in front of the couch*) Oh, no, Will, that's my uncle. He's not here this weekend.

MARY   Oh, then it was you who was waving.

LEE   No, that was my brother, Owen. He just stepped out.

MARY   Oh. Well, it looked like he was trying to tell us something, but we couldn't make out what he was saying.

LEE   (*embarrassed*) Yeah, well, it was nothing. Just boat things, you know. Ship ahoy.

MARY   I see.

LEE   (*moving to MARY, to shake her hand*) I'm sorry, I'm Lee. Lee Melville.

MARY   Mary.

LEE   So, you know Uncle Will, do you?

MARY   Yes, I own that little store up the road, so I know just about everybody around here.

LEE   Oh, that's where Owen is now. You're not closed are you? I mean, with you here.

MARY   No, it's open. My mother looks after the store most of the time.

LEE   Oh.

MARY   Well, I'd better get going. My sister's waiting down by the boat. Sorry to bother you. (*moves left*)

LEE   Oh, no bother. I'm just sorry you came all the way in for nothing.

LORETTA   (*offstage*) Shit!!

LEE   Is... uh... is that your sister?

MARY   I'm afraid so.

LORETTA   (*offstage*) Goddamn it!! Mary!

MARY   What?

> *LORETTA enters the porch. She is about twenty-five and dressed a little sharper than MARY, in more fashionable outdoor clothing. She too wears a life jacket.*

LORETTA   Mary, the boat got away.

MARY   What do you mean, it got away?

LORETTA   I guess I didn't tie it up right. I don't know. It just got away.

LEE   I'll get it. (*rushes out left*)

MARY   No, I can get it.

LEE   (*exiting*) It's okay.

MARY   What's the matter with you, Loretta? Don't you know how to tie a boat up yet?

LORETTA   (*entering the cabin*) Hey, I'm not Popeye!

MARY	Well, you'd better hope he can get it back.
LORETTA	(*sitting on the couch*) Get it back? I hope I never see that stupid boat again. Look at my shoe. It's soaking wet. It's ruined! (*takes her shoe off*)
MARY	Oh, it's not ruined. It's a deck shoe, for heaven's sake. It's supposed to get wet.
LORETTA	Oh, yeah, well I paid forty-five dollars for these, and I don't get anything wet that costs forty-five dollars. (*moves to the wood stove right and feels the top of it*) Great. No heat. So, how am I supposed to get it dry? Stupid damn boat!
MARY	Oh, don't start with the boat again.
LORETTA	(*moving left towards MARY*) Well, really, Mary. Don't you think there's something wrong when two grown women have to depend on a boat as their only means of transportation?
MARY	No, I don't.
LORETTA	Well, I do. I mean, somebody went to a helluva lot of trouble to carve roads out of this Godforsaken country. I think the least we can do is use them.
MARY	There's nothing wrong with riding in a boat.
LORETTA	There is too. It's just not... attractive. Look at us. We look like Tweedledee and Tweedledum. I think it's time one of us bought a car.
MARY	One of us?
LORETTA	Well, I'll chip in a bit too. (*exits to bedroom right*)
MARY	Look, if you want a car that badly, why don't you ask your friend Harry Farmer to give you one?
LORETTA	(*poking her head out*) Harry doesn't give cars away. He sells them. (*goes back inside*)

MARY   Oh, but Harry likes you. He's always phoning you...
              asking you out on a date. I'll bet he'd give you one if
              you married him.

LORETTA   (*bursting out of the bedroom angrily*) That is not funny,
              Mary. Harry is slime. Our relationship is strictly
              business. (*turns toward the bathroom*) So, who's the
              guy chasing our boat? (*opens the bathroom door and
              goes in*)

MARY   It's Will's nephew. He and his brother are using the
              cabin. (*notices LORETTA in the bathroom*) Loretta,
              what are you doing?

LORETTA   (*poking her head out again*) I'm looking for a blow
              dryer. I'm not leaving here until this shoe is dry.
              (*enters the bathroom again*)

MARY   (*moving to the bathroom*) Loretta, you shouldn't be
              snooping in other people's bathrooms when they're
              not around.

LORETTA   (*offstage*) I'm not snooping.

MARY   (*entering the bathroom*) Loretta, come out of there.

              *OWEN enters upstage centre. He is carrying a bag of
              groceries.*

OWEN   Honey. I'm home!

              *The bathroom door slams. OWEN looks behind him to
              the door upstage centre. OWEN closes the door.
              MARY enters from the bathroom, embarrassed.*

MARY   Hello. You must be Owen. I'm Mary.

              *MARY moves straight across to the screen door, left.
              OWEN says nothing. He just stares in disbelief.*

LORETTA   (*entering from the bathroom*) Hi.

              OWEN looks at LORETTA. Still saying nothing.

Are you one of the guys staying here?

OWEN   Huh?

LORETTA   Have you got a blow dryer around here anywhere?

OWEN   A what?

LORETTA   A blow dryer. Have you got one?

OWEN   Uh... no.

LORETTA   Shit. (*moves into the kitchen area*)

OWEN   Sorry. (*looks into the bathroom, cautiously, half expecting to see more girls inside*)

LORETTA   (*putting her shoe into the oven*) Oh, well, I guess we'll just have to do it this way. One-fifty should be enough. (*sets the dial*)

MARY   (*to OWEN*) This is my sister, Loretta.

OWEN   Hi.

LORETTA   Whatcha got?

OWEN   Huh?

LORETTA   In the bag.

OWEN   Oh... uh, breakfast. (*beat*) Did you want some?

LORETTA   No thanks.

LEE   (*entering through the screen door left*) Well, I got it.

OWEN   Lee. Look what I found.

LEE   I see you've met my brother.

MARY   Yes. Did you have any trouble?

LEE   Not really. It drifted back into shore a little ways down.

MARY   Oh, well, thank you very much. (*opens the screen door and steps into the porch, anxious to leave*)

OWEN   (*suddenly dawning on him*) Hey. You're the girls in the boat. Yeah. You were out there. And I was waving to you. Right there. Did you see me?

MARY   Yes, we did.

OWEN   Well, how 'bout that? And you came up. (*looks at LEE with pride*)

LEE   Owen...

OWEN   Listen, I'm sorry I wasn't here when you got here, but I didn't think you'd come up, and I had to go to the store. (*moves to the kitchen area and sets the groceries down*) I would've been back sooner, but the old lady who runs the store up there is kinda slow. She didn't know where anything was. I think her mind's starting to go.

MARY   (*opens the screen door and steps back inside, slowly*) Well, Mom is getting on in years.

OWEN   Mom? Is that what they call her?

MARY   No, that's what we call her.

OWEN   Oh? Why's that?

LORETTA   Because she's our mother.

OWEN   (*stares at LORETTA for what seems like an eternity*) Oh. (*looks over to LEE*) So, who wants a beer? (*goes to the fridge*)

MARY   Oh, no thanks. We'd better be going.

OWEN   Going? (*moves downstage to MARY*)

LORETTA   Mary, my shoe isn't done yet.

OWEN   Yeah, you just got here. *I* just got here.

MARY   Well, we don't want to keep you.

OWEN   Keep us? Keep us from what? We got no plans. Right, Lee?

LEE   Well, actually, we were going to go fishing.

OWEN   Fishing? Already? It's only noon! The fish don't start biting 'til three, four o'clock. Come on, Mary. Stick around for a while. Have a beer. Chew the fat.

LORETTA   I'll have a beer. Anything to keep me out of that boat.

OWEN   Now you're talking. (*moves to the fridge*) Mary? One for you too?

MARY   Well

OWEN   Attagirl. Go on in. Sit down. Take a load off.

> *LORETTA gives MARY a gentle shove towards the couch. MARY goes and sits down.*

Lee? How 'bout you? You want one?

LEE   No thanks.

OWEN   You sure?

LEE   Yes, I'm sure.

> *LORETTA checks on her shoe in the oven. OWEN wants LEE to strike up a conversation with MARY. He pushes him towards the couch. LEE resists. OWEN pushes again. LEE moves right, behind the couch. OWEN moves to LORETTA. LEE picks up a newspaper.*

Uh... so, I see the Cougars lost another one.

MARY   I beg your pardon?

LEE   The Cougars. The football team. They lost another game.

MARY   Oh. That's too bad.

LEE   Well, it's early yet. (*sits in the rocking chair, right*) They've still got a lot of football to play. We'll just have to wait and see how they do later on.

MARY   I suppose.

LEE   Yeah, no need to panic yet.

MARY   (*after an awkward pause*) Do you go to many games?

LEE   What games?

MARY   Well, the football games.

LEE   Oh, yeah, yeah. We go all the time. We've got season's tickets, so we go to all the games.... Well, all the home games. We don't go on the road with the team. Just, uh... just the home games. (*in a panic*) Owen, how's Mary's beer coming?

OWEN   (*concentrating on LORETTA*) Be right there.

LEE   (*to MARY*) It'll be right here. (*awkward pause*) The service is terrible in this place.

     MARY and LEE laugh nervously. As his laugh dies down, LEE pleads once more.

     Owen?

OWEN   Okay, here we go. That's one for Lorraine. (*hands LORETTA a beer*)

LORETTA   Loretta.

OWEN   Loretta, right. That's a real nice name. (*moves downstage*)

LORETTA   Thanks. I think my mother wanted me to be a
           country singer.

OWEN   Is that right?

           OWEN hands MARY her beer.

           How about you, Mary? What'd your mother want
           you to be?

           MARY just looks up at him.

LORETTA   Mom wanted Mary to be little Miss Perfect. Isn't that
           right, Mary?

MARY   Thank you, Loretta.

LORETTA   (*moving behind the couch*) Oh, Mary, I'm sorry. I've
           embarrassed you.

MARY   No. you didn't.

           *OWEN moves behind LORETTA and stands beside
           the rocking chair.*

LORETTA   Mary was the original nice girl. Mom was so proud
           of her. Mary, do you remember the night you ran
           home crying from the school dance, because Gilbert
           Sweeny kept sliding his hand down the back of you
           while you were dancing?

MARY   He had sweaty palms.

LORETTA   I mean, *me*, I thought that was the way you were
           supposed to dance. I still do.

OWEN   (*aside to LEE*) That one's mine.

LEE   (*gives OWEN a slap on the leg*) Uh so, have you lived
           up here long?

MARY   Well, I've been here for about five years, and Mom
           and Loretta moved up about, what, a year and a half
           ago, Loretta?

LORETTA   I'd rather not think about it. (*moves upstage, to the counter where the rifle is lying*)

MARY   About a year and a half ago.

LORETTA   (*picking up the gun delicately by the barrel*) Hey, you guys aren't hunters, are you?

OWEN   Huh? (*moves left to her*)

LORETTA   Is that what you do with this thing? Shoot defenseless animals?

OWEN   What, us? Bite your tongue.

>   OWEN *takes the gun from* LORETTA.

We're not hunters. As a matter of fact, nobody in our family hunts. We don't believe in that sort of thing.

LORETTA   Is that right? So, what happened to him? (*points to the deer head*) Suicide?

OWEN   (*setting the gun down*) Uh... no, that was Uncle Will did that. He's not really family. He's married to my aunt.

MARY   So, what do you fellas do for a living?

LEE   Well, we work at Hudson Plastics right now.

MARY   Oh.

OWEN   Yeah, Lee's the foreman there. Looks after the whole operation.

LEE   Well, it's not much really.

OWEN   Not much? Listen to him, will ya? He's only got about a hundred guys under him. Not much.

MARY   (*to* OWEN) And what do you do there?

OWEN   Me? Well, I guess you could call me Lee's right hand
            man. I do all his dirty work for him. Right, Lee? You
            know, keep an eye on things. Make sure nobody's
            slackin' off.

LORETTA   What's Hudson Plastics?

OWEN   Well, it's a factory. We make things. Like those big
            plastic garbage cans. Or those plastic flower pots
            that you see in the K-Mart all the time.

LORETTA   (not really interested) Oh, so you're the ones who
            make those.

OWEN   Yeah. Say, listen, I can get you all the flower pots
            you want. Just give me a call at work sometime and
            I'll put a few aside for you. On the house.

LORETTA   No thanks. I'm not really into flowers.

OWEN   (enthusiasm dampened) Oh.... Well, how about garbage
            cans? You need any of those?

LEE   (standing) Well, I suppose you two are in a hurry to
            get back to your store. We really shouldn't keep you.

OWEN   Oh, do you girls work at the store too?

MARY   Well, actually, I own it.

OWEN   You own it?

MARY   Yes.

LORETTA   And I only work there once in a while. It's just
            temporary until I can get my acting career off the
            ground.

OWEN   Acting? You're an actress?

LORETTA   Yes. I act in television commercials.

OWEN   Oh.

LORETTA   That's where the real money is. I mean, I could live quite comfortably by making ten or fifteen commercials a year.

OWEN   Wow. How many have you made?

LORETTA   Oh, I don't remember exactly.

MARY   I think it's two, isn't it, dear?

LORETTA   Uh, yes, something like that. Maybe a few more.

MARY   No, no, I'm pretty sure it's two.

LORETTA   Uh-huh. Well, you're probably close. It's around that.

MARY   (*to LEE*) Yes, it's two.

LORETTA   (*irritated*) All right! It's two. (*to OWEN*) Of course, right now I'm under exclusive contract to Harry Farmer's Used Car Showroom, and that sort of ties me down.

OWEN   Can you show us one?

LORETTA   One what? A commercial?

OWEN   Yeah, do one for us right here.

LORETTA   No, I couldn't do one here.

OWEN   Aw, come on.

LORETTA   No, the lighting's all wrong in here. And I have to have a car to stand beside.

OWEN   Come on. Please?

LEE   Owen, she doesn't want to do it. Now, we've kept these ladies from their business long enough. I think we should just let them be on their way.

LORETTA   All right. The couch can be the car. Get up, Mary. (*to OWEN*) I'll need my shoe.

           OWEN goes to the oven to get the shoe.

           Come on, Mary, get up. You're sitting on the car.

           MARY moves to the rocking chair, right.

OWEN   (*bringing the shoe to LORETTA*) Here we go.

LORETTA   (*holding out her hand*) Thanks.

OWEN   No, let me do it for you.

           LORETTA sits on the couch. OWEN straddles her legs and pulls her foot up, causing her to slide down on the couch. He puts the shoe on her foot.

           How's this for service? Just like Cinderella.

LORETTA   Funny, I feel more like Secretariat.

           OWEN drops her leg and hurries to the fridge to get a beer. Then he pulls out one of the chairs at the table, and moves it down where he can get a clear view of LORETTA who has moved around behind the couch.

           Now, when the commercial starts, I'm standing behind the car, looking right into the camera. And behind me here is the showroom, with a big sign in the window that says "Priced to Clear." You got that?

OWEN   Got it. Priced to clear.

LORETTA   Okay. And then I start. (*beat*) Hi (*walks downstage to the front of the couch as she talks*) This is Loretta Starr, for Harry Farmer's Used Car Showroom. (*to OWEN*) Starr isn't my real name. Harry thinks it sounds better.

OWEN   I like it. Sounds great.

LORETTA   (*rushing around to the back of the couch again*) Okay. (*beat*) Hi! (*strolls downstage to the front of the couch again*) This is Loretta Starr, for Harry Farmer's Used Car Showroom. And now, here's Harry to tell you all about this 1977 Dodge Dart.

> *LORETTA swings her arm back as if introducing Harry. OWEN looks upstage left to where LEE is standing by the fridge. LEE, in turn, looks to his left, half expecting to see Harry Farmer appear.*

Well, come on.

LEE   What? Me?

LORETTA   Yeah. You have to be Harry.

LEE   No. I don't know anything about commercials.

LORETTA   That doesn't matter. Your part's easy.

LEE   No, really...

OWEN   Go on, Lee.

LEE   No...

LORETTA   Well, I can't do it unless you're Harry.

OWEN   (*standing, and speaking sternly*) Do it, Lee.

LEE   Well...

LORETTA   Oh, hurry up. Come on.

LEE   Well, all right. (*moves downstage to LORETTA*) But, I'm warning you, I won't be very good.

LORETTA   That's okay. Harry's not very good either. Now, you stand right here beside me.

> *LORETTA stands LEE in place.*

That's it. Right there. Okay. All set?

LEE   I guess so.

LORETTA   Good. Now, tell them about the car. (*strikes her best model's pose*)

LEE   What?

LORETTA   The Dodge Dart. Tell them about it.

LEE   (*turns his back to look at the couch*) Well, let's see here...

    LORETTA grabs LEE and turns him around again.

LORETTA   And don't forget. You have to make love to the camera while you're doing it.

LEE   Do what?

LORETTA   The camera. You have to play to it. The sexual thing is very important here.

    At this point, OWEN pops open his can of beer, and it spurts into the air.

    You see, the idea is that you have to seduce the female viewers, and I have to seduce the men.

OWEN   Damn, this is good.

LORETTA   Okay, go ahead. Sell the car. (*strikes her pose again*)

LEE   Uh... well.... It's maroon. It seats three. And it's scotch-guarded.

    LORETTA moves in, puts her arm around LEE, and looks into the imaginary camera.

LORETTA   So, get down here today friends. Harry Farmer's Used Car Showroom. Just below the tracks on St. Charles. We'll be waiting.

    LORETTA waves. LEE is watching her and he waves.

    And then we smile.

> *LEE smiles, still looking at LORETTA. LORETTA turns his head toward the camera.*

At the camera. And that's it.

OWEN   (*getting up and moving right*) Oh! Oh! I don't mind telling you, that blew me away! That was really something. Wasn't that something, Mary?

MARY   Oh, it was something all right. (*rises*) Time to go, Loretta.

> *LEE goes to the sink to get a cloth to wipe up the beer on the floor.*

OWEN   Oh, no, not yet. Do one more for us.

MARY   (*moving to LORETTA and escorting her, left*) No, please, don't get her started.

OWEN   Aw, just one more?

LEE   (*on the floor, wiping the beer*) Forget it, Owen. You couldn't stand the excitement.

MARY   We really can't stay. We're on our way to the Legion Hall to help them get set up for the dance tonight.

OWEN   Dance? There's a dance tonight?

MARY   Yes. Actually, it's a pot luck supper, and then a dance. You know, everybody brings a dish.

OWEN   We should go, Lee.

LEE   Oh, I don't think so. (*moves upstage to the sink*)

OWEN   Sure, it'll be fun.

LEE   No, we haven't got any food to bring.

LORETTA   Oh, you don't have to bring any food. There'll be plenty there.

OWEN   There you go. We don't have to bring food.

LEE   No, I... I didn't bring any clothes to wear to a dance.

OWEN   It's the Legion for godsake! We'll pin a couple of fishing lures to our shirts. They'll think we're war heroes.

LEE   No, I don't know. We wouldn't know anybody there.

OWEN   We'll go with Mary and Loretta. We know them.

LEE   Owen, we can't just invite ourselves to go with Mary and Loretta. They've probably got dates already. (*to the girls*) You've probably got dates already, right?

   MARY and LORETTA shake their heads.

OWEN   Well, all right then. (*moves close to LORETTA*) Would you like to go with us? You know, we'll have a few yuks. Put on the feedbag.

LORETTA   (*to MARY*) Hard for a girl to say no when he puts it like that.

LEE   Owen, I really think we're imposing here.

LORETTA   Leave him alone. (*to OWEN*) Have you got a car?

OWEN   Yeah.

LORETTA   You're on.

OWEN   Terrific. How's that sound to you, Mary?

MARY   (*looking at LEE*) Well... if everyone else agrees.

LEE   Uh... Owen, could I speak to you for a moment?

OWEN   Sure. What is it?

LEE   In the bedroom. (*moves to the bedroom, right*)

OWEN   What's the matter?

LEE	Nothing. I just want to talk to you. Just for a minute.
OWEN	(*moving to the bedroom door*) All right, but this is very rude, Lee. We do have guests.
MARY	Listen, maybe we should leave.
LEE	Oh, no. Don't go yet. Please. This shouldn't take long. Just make yourself comfortable. We'll be right back.

> *LEE pushes OWEN into the bedroom, and closes the door.*

What the hell's the matter with you?

OWEN	(*offstage*) What did I do?

> *OWEN and LEE's conversation continues in whispers. LORETTA runs to the cupboard and grabs a glass and then rushes to the bedroom door.*

LORETTA	Oh, I'll bet this is going to be good.
MARY	Loretta, what are you doing?
LORETTA	(*holding the glass to the door to hear better*) Shhhh! Listen.
MARY	Come away from there.
LORETTA	Oh, they're really going at it.
MARY	Loretta, that is a private conversation. You shouldn't be eavesdropping.
LORETTA	He says he doesn't want to go.
MARY	Why? (*moves to the bedroom door*)
LORETTA	He's married.
MARY	Well, I knew he had to have a good reason.

LORETTA   Wait a minute, wait a minute.... The other one is
            starting to beg now.... Yeah... yeah. Oh, he's really
            crawling, Mary. This is great.

MARY   (*moving left*) Come on, Loretta. Let's go.

LORETTA   Wait. Don't you want to see how it turns out?

MARY   No. Do you want to spend the evening with a date
            who doesn't even want to be with you?

LORETTA   No. I was kind of hoping he'd be your date.

MARY   Well, he's not going to be. Now, come on.

LORETTA   (*moving to MARY*) No, Mary. I think this is what you
            need. I mean, how long has it been since you've
            been out with a guy?

MARY   That's got nothing to do with it. He doesn't want to
            go.

LORETTA   So, that just makes it more of a challenge.

MARY   Loretta, he's married.

LORETTA   So are you. It's perfect! Come on, Mary. Where's
            your sense of adventure?

MARY   Having you for a sister is all the adventure I need,
            Loretta. (*moves for the screen door, left*)

LORETTA   You're afraid, aren't you?

MARY   (*stopping again*) Afraid of what?

LORETTA   You know. You're afraid that maybe the old magic
            isn't there anymore.

MARY   The old magic was never there.

LORETTA   Oh, don't give me that, Mary. You had it. I used to
            watch you. The way you worked on all those boys. I
            mean, they never got anywhere with you, but you
            made them think it was an honour just to try.

MARY   (*smiling*) Are you coming, or not? (*opens the screen door*)

LORETTA   (*sets the glass on the table*) Well, I suppose it's only natural to feel that way, I mean, considering your age and all. (*exits to the porch*)

MARY   Hold it, blondie.

              LORETTA stops.

MARY   Are you saying that I'm not attractive to men anymore?

LORETTA   No, not exactly.

MARY   You don't think a man would enjoy my company?

LORETTA   Well, that depends on the man. (*moves back into the room*)

MARY   Is that right? And I suppose at my age, I wouldn't be much of a date, is that it?

LORETTA   Now, I didn't say that.

              The bedroom door opens and OWEN and LEE enter.

OWEN   Okay, what time should we pick you up?

MARY   Seven o'clock. And don't be late. (*starts to exit, left*)

OWEN   Wait a minute.

              MARY stops.

              On second thought, why don't you meet us here at seven, and then we'll go in the car from here?

LORETTA   Meet you? That means we'll have to come over in the boat.

OWEN   Well, it's just that it's been a long time since we've been in the area, and I'm afraid we might get lost.

LORETTA   (*whining to MARY*) He wants us to come over in the boat.

MARY   That'll be fine. Come on, Loretta.

> *MARY pulls LORETTA left and they exit through the screen door.*

LORETTA   (*as MARY pulls her out of the cabin and offstage*) But, Mary, I don't want to come over in the goddamn boat.

> *OWEN follows them as far as the porch. Then he moves back right, very pleased with himself.*

OWEN   I think we impressed the hell out of them. Don't you?

LEE   (*moving upstage to the kitchen area*) Just remember, Owen. Nothing happens. We take them to the dance and then we take them straight home.

OWEN   Hey, absolutely. Absolutely. (*beat*) Well, we can't take them straight home. I mean, they'll have to come back here to get their boat. But, after that, they go straight home. (*turns and looks out the screen door again*) Boy, I like that Loretta. I mean, we really hit it off. Did you notice? (*moves to the table and sits*) And you know, I think maybe you and Mary could have something going there too.

LEE   Me and Mary? We hardly spoke.

OWEN   Yeah, I know, but just for a second there, I thought I saw something. You know... kind of a... look in her eye.

LEE   Get out of here. A look in her eye.

OWEN   It was probably nothing.

LEE   It was nothing. I'm warning you, Owen. If Arlene ever finds out about this...

OWEN   How's she going to find out? She's two hundred miles away.

LEE   She'll find out. She can sense these things. I'll bet she knows right now. She's probably on her way up here.

OWEN   (*rising*) She's not going to find out. Now, will you stop worrying. I'm going to go check the boat out. Don't be long. (*exits left*)

LEE   (*moving to the screen door and calling after OWEN*) Hey, you owe me one, Owen! I'm only doing this for you, you know! (*to himself*) A look in her eye. We didn't say two words to each other. (*beat, yells out the door*) All right, so what the hell kind of look was this?! (*moves out into the porch*) Owen! (*exits left*)

SCENE 3

        Later that night. The cabin. As the scene opens, there is no one onstage. There are a few empty beer cans around. One of the girls' life jackets is on the couch. The other is on the back of a kitchen chair. LEE and MARY enter upstage centre. LEE turns on the light switch just inside the door, and the lights come up. LEE is now wearing a different shirt, and MARY wears a dress. She carries a cake in a Tupperware container. MARY moves downstage and puts the cake on the table.

LEE   I'm telling you, the reason nobody touched your cake is that meal. It was too filling. Nobody had any room left. I'm still full myself. (*hangs up his coat upstage right*)

MARY   Well, it's nice of you to say that, but, the truth is, I just never learned how to cook, that's all.

LEE   No, that's not it.

MARY   That's all right. It doesn't bother me. I mean, there are more important things than knowing how to cook, right?

LEE   Listen, I'll have a piece right now. (*moves to the table left*)

MARY   I thought you were full.

LEE   Well, I think I should prove you wrong about your cooking. What kind of cake is it? (*runs his finger across the top of the cake and puts a bit in his mouth*)

MARY   Turnip.

LEE   (*freezes, finger still in mouth*) Turnip? I can't ever recall having turnip cake before.

MARY   I found the recipe in one of those vegetarian survival books.

LEE   Is that right? Well, what'll they think of next? (*moves downstage and wipes the cake off on his pants*)

MARY   Do you still want some? (*moves upstage centre and takes two small plates out of the cupboard*)

LEE   Uh... yeah. In a while. I'll just let this meal settle first.

MARY   (*sets the plates on the counter, and moves downstage*) So, did you have a good time tonight?

LEE   Yeah, it was all right.

MARY   Just all right? I mean, you seemed to be having fun. We danced a lot.

LEE   Well, that was just so I wouldn't have to talk to anyone there. I'm not very good at making small talk with strangers.

MARY   Oh, I see.

LEE   Well, don't misunderstand me now. It wasn't awful. I didn't have a horrible time. It was pretty good.

MARY   (*with a false smile*) Well, as long as it wasn't hell for you, that's all that matters.

LEE   No, I didn't mean it like that. It was fine. Really.

            LORETTA is yelling and laughing offstage.

LORETTA   (*offstage*) Stop it, Owen! Stop it!

LEE   What's he doing now? (*moves to the door upstage centre*) Owen, put her down! I said, put her down!

MARY   What's going on?

LEE   (*coming back inside*) I think he's trying to guess your sister's weight.

MARY   He's what?

LEE   Yeah, he says it's an ice breaker.

            LORETTA enters upstage centre. She is wearing a dress. OWEN follows closely behind.

OWEN   So was I close, or what?

LORETTA   No. (*moves down right, around in front of the couch*)

OWEN   It's not a hundred and ten. One fifteen then.

LORETTA   No.

OWEN   Maybe I wasn't holding all of you. Let me try again.

            OWEN picks up LORETTA.

LEE   Owen, leave her alone. She's got a dress on.

OWEN   You're right. This should actually be done without the benefit of clothing. (*to LORETTA*) What do you say?

            OWEN sits on the couch, with LORETTA on his lap.

LORETTA   Boy, you never stop, do you?

OWEN   Are you kidding? (*stands*) I'm just getting warmed up.

> OWEN *moves up, to the kitchen area. He looks at MARY and then, sadly, at the cake.*

Gee, Mary, I'm awful sorry nobody liked your cake. (*pauses, trying to control a snicker*) Are there really turnips in there?

LEE   Owen, it wasn't that nobody liked it.

OWEN   No? What was it then?

MARY   The meal was too filling.

LEE   Exactly. Nobody had any room left for dessert.

OWEN   Oh. Right. (*winks at LEE*) Why didn't I think of that? (*moves back downstage and flops on the couch*)

MARY   Loretta, it's getting late. Maybe we should be going now.

LEE   (*looking at his watch*) Oh boy. Is it that late already?

MARY   Well, you know how time flies. (*picks up her life jacket off the chair*) Loretta?

OWEN   Now, wait a minute, now. It's barely midnight. Stick around for a while. Have a beer. Who wants a beer? Loretta? (*gets up again and moves to the refrigerator*)

LORETTA   No, thanks.

OWEN   Mary?

MARY   No, thank you.

OWEN   Lee?

LEE   No, thanks.

OWEN   Okay, that's four beer. (*opens up the fridge and takes out a string of cans*)

LORETTA   (*getting up and moving upstage centre*) I know what I want. I want to go for a swim.

LEE   A swim? Now?

LORETTA   Sure. It'll be refreshing.

MARY   Loretta, I think it's rather cool for a swim.

LORETTA   No, it's not. It's perfect. (*facing OWEN*) I just love the feeling of cool water washing over my warm body by moonlight. It makes me tingle everywhere. (*moves to the screen door left*)

OWEN   (*turned on*) Mercy. (*drops the beer*)

LORETTA   (*stopping at the screen door*) Anybody else coming? (*exits, left*)

OWEN   (*visibly shaken*) Hey... wait a minute. (*moves slowly to the screen door*) I thought we could sit around in here for a while. You know... shoot the breeze... have some beer... get to know each other... (*as he reaches the screen door, his lust gets the better of him*) Oh, God, I like that girl! (*quickly exits, left*)

LEE   (*moving left, to the door*) Owen? Owen! (*to MARY*) He shouldn't be doing that, you know. He's getting married in less than a month. (*yelling*) Owen? (*to MARY*) I thought your sister didn't like the water.

MARY   (*moving right*) Oh, she doesn't mind swimming in it. It's riding on top of it she doesn't like. (*sits on the couch*)

LEE   Well, does she know she's out there with an engaged man?

MARY   Oh, I don't think it would matter if she did.

LEE   You mean, she doesn't care? (*picks up the beer that OWEN dropped, and puts it back in the fridge*)

MARY   Well, actually, Loretta only really cares about Loretta. I've always envied her for that.

LEE   Envied her? For being selfish?

MARY   Sure. It's easier to make decisions that way. You just decide to do what's best for you, and you don't worry about how it affects anybody else. Don't you think it would be easier that way?

LEE   (*moving to look out the screen door again*) I wouldn't know.

MARY   Of course you wouldn't. You've never tried it.

LEE   (*moving right, towards MARY*) What makes you say that?

MARY   Oh, I can tell.

LEE   How?

MARY   Well, for instance, you didn't want to go to the dance tonight, but you went because your brother wanted to go. I got the feeling you didn't want us around this morning, but you didn't kick us out. And you probably don't want us here right now, but you haven't asked us to leave.

LEE   Is that right? Well, I'll have you know I can be pretty selfish when I want to be.

MARY   No, I don't think so.

LEE   (*moving right and sitting beside MARY*) Oh, yes I can. As a matter of fact, I did something tonight that was selfish. Something that was in my best interest.

MARY   And what was that?

LEE   I didn't eat any of your cake.

MARY and LEE both laugh.

MARY   You're right. That was selfish.

An awkward pause. LEE gets up and moves back to the screen door left.

Anyway, it looks like we're stuck here for a while. At least until those two cool off. (*gets up and moves to LEE*) So, what do you want to do?

LEE   (*nervously*) Do?

MARY   Yeah. You want to do something?

LEE   Listen, I should tell you that I'm a married man.

MARY   (*slightly offended*) Well, I guess that rules out getting married then, doesn't it? You want to play cards? (*moves upstage, behind the table*)

LEE   I'm sorry. I don't know why I said that.

MARY   (*getting a fork from the cupboard upstage centre*) It was a very innocent question.

LEE   I know. I guess I was just protecting myself.

MARY   From what? From me? The original nice girl? (*picks up one of the plates off the counter and sets it on the table*)

LEE   I don't know. Maybe.

MARY   Well, listen, I'm married too.

LEE   (*relieved*) Oh. I didn't know that.

MARY   You didn't ask. (*moves upstage, to the fridge*)

LEE   So, where's your husband tonight?

MARY   I'm not sure. (*opens the fridge and takes out a beer*)

LEE	Well, is he out of town?
MARY	Oh, he's out of town all right. (*holding up the beer*) Do you mind?
LEE	No, go ahead.
MARY	You see, technically I'm still married. He left me two years ago. (*moves to the table and sits; cuts herself a piece of cake and puts it on the plate*)
LEE	Oh, I'm sorry.
MARY	Yeah, me too.
LEE	Why did he leave? (*sits at the table*)
MARY	I don't know. He didn't tell me.
LEE	He didn't tell you why?
MARY	He didn't tell me he was leaving. I woke up one morning and he was gone. He left me a note saying he'd send some money for the car.
LEE	He took the car too?
MARY	(*affirmative*) Hm-hmm. Oh, I don't blame him for that. I mean, if I was going to leave, I'd take the car.

> MARY takes a bite of the cake, and then tries to hide the fact that it tastes awful. LEE, smiling, opens her beer for her and places it in front of her. She takes a drink.

LEE	So, do you have any idea where he is?
MARY	Who?
LEE	Your husband.
MARY	Oh. Uh, well, he's probably down south somewhere. He always said he wanted to move south. I would've moved with him, but he never asked.

LEE	Well, if you don't mind my saying so, this guy sounds like a jerk.
MARY	Yeah, I thought so too, at the time.
LEE	And what about now?
MARY	Now? Now, I wish he'd come back.
LEE	Come back? You wouldn't take him back?
MARY	Sure. Why not?
LEE	After all this time? After the way he left?
MARY	I miss him. I guess I still love him.
LEE	The man took your car! He didn't tell you he was leaving. He didn't even have the decency to tell you why!
MARY	I think he felt trapped.
LEE	Oh, come on. That's the oldest excuse in the world. Everybody feels trapped. Don't you think I feel trapped once in a while?
MARY	How should I know? I met you this morning.
LEE	Well, I do. A lot of the time!
MARY	So, why don't you leave?
LEE	We're not talking about me. We're talking about your husband. (*stands, and starts to pace*) I can't believe you'd take him back. Is this what you've been doing for the past two years? Sitting around waiting for this clown to come home with your car?
MARY	You know, you're taking this harder than I did.
LEE	He's probably sold the car. You realize that. I mean, as far as he's concerned, it's party time. And that's what you should be thinking too. You should forget him. Find somebody else. Start dating.

MARY   Who says I haven't been dating?

LEE   Not if you're still waiting for him, you haven't been.

MARY   Well, what about tonight?

LEE   What about tonight?

MARY   Isn't this a date?

LEE   (*getting nervous again*) What... this? You mean, you and me? No, this is not a date.

MARY   Well, what is it then?

LEE   Uh... well... it's more like a car pool.

MARY   A car pool?!! (*gets up and storms to the couch*)

LEE   Well, no, not a car pool. It's more like... like you and I are chaperoning Owen and Loretta. (*moves to the screen door left and yells out*) Hey, are you two behaving yourselves out there?!

MARY   (*putting on her life jacket*) All right, don't worry about it. It's not a date. I'm too old for this silly dating business anyway.

LEE   (*moving right*) Too old? No, you're not. No. You should get out there. Meet somebody. Somebody who appreciates you .

MARY   I already had somebody who appreciated me. At least, I thought he did. And look what happened.

LEE   So, find somebody else.

MARY   What, and make the same mistake again? No thank you.

LEE   Look, all I'm saying is, it's a waste. A waste of a terrific person. You shouldn't be alone.

MARY   I can get by alone.

LEE   Oh, sure you can get by. Anybody can *get by*, if that's
            all you want to do is *get by*! Is that all you want to
            do? Is that how you want to be remembered? As the
            girl who got by?! "What kind of a girl was Mary,
            anyway? Oh, she got by. Was she a smart girl? Well,
            she got by. How was she at sex? Oh, she got by."

MARY   I think I'd better go.

            *MARY starts to move left but LEE stops her with his
            next speech.*

LEE   You know what's worse than your husband leaving
            you? It's you, sitting around waiting for him to come
            back. Yeah, I'll tell you this. After I'm gone, Arlene's
            not going to sit around for long. No sir. She'll start
            dating, and in a few years she'll be married again.
            And she's older than you are, I'll bet. How old are
            you?

MARY   Thirty-one.

LEE   There you go. Arlene's thirty-three.

MARY   What are you saying? Are you telling me you *are*
            leaving?

LEE   (*moving back to the table*) No, I'm not leaving. I'm
            dying. And I don't want that to ruin Arlene's life.
            Look, you said you wanted to be a little more selfish.
            Well, now's a good time to start. Start doing what's
            best for you. (*sits at the table*)

MARY   (*after a pause*) Can we back up here for just a second.
            Did you say "I'm dying?"

LEE   (*trying to cover it up now*) Uh... I don't know. Maybe
            I did.

MARY   Yeah, well, I think you did. I'm pretty sure I heard
            "I'm dying" in there somewhere.

LEE   All right, I said it. Let's just forget it, okay?
            Sometimes I get stuck for something to say, so
            I just blurt anything out.

MARY   You get stuck for something to say, so you say "I'm
           dying?" I mean, I thought the conversation was
           going along fine. You were more than holding up
           your end. Didn't you think it was going along fine?

LEE   Yes, I did...

MARY   Well, then, what the hell's "I'm dying" supposed to
           mean?

LEE   I don't know why I said it. Maybe you seemed like
           the kind of person I could say it to without getting
           emotional.

MARY   Without who getting emotional?

LEE   You!... and me. Both of us. I'd just like to talk about
           it once without somebody crying. I talk to my
           mother about it, and she cries. I talk to Arlene about
           it... she cries. And Owen, well, he won't talk about it
           at all. I mean, I figured, you're not involved... you
           hardly know me. What's to cry about? Right? I'm
           sorry. I shouldn't have brought it up. We won't talk
           about it anymore, okay?

MARY   (quietly) Okay.

LEE   Okay.

MARY   (after a short pause, trying to hold back the tears) You
           really are dying, aren't you?

LEE   No.

MARY   Yes you are.

LEE   No, I'm not. I lied.

MARY   No, you are. You really are. (puts her hand over her
           mouth to stifle her next line) Oh, my God. (turns away
           from Lee and takes a Kleenex out of the box on the shelf,
           left)

LEE   What are you doing?

MARY	Nothing. (*on the verge of breaking down*)
LEE	What have you got there?
MARY	Nothing.
LEE	Is that a Kleenex? (*stands up*)
MARY	No. (*moves upstage to the stove, her back still turned to LEE*)
LEE	It is. It's a Kleenex. What's it for?
MARY	It's for nothing.
LEE	No, it's for something. You don't just pick up a Kleenex for nothing.
MARY	Yes, you do.
LEE	No, you don't. Now, what's it for? Are you getting emotional?
MARY	No.
LEE	You are, aren't you? You're crying.
MARY	(*turns to him in a tearful outburst*) I am not!!
LEE	(*turning away*) Oh, God, not another one.
MARY	Well, I can't help it. I'm an emotional person.
LEE	But, we're practically strangers.
MARY	We've dated.
LEE	We haven't dated! This is not a date!!
MARY	(*sitting at the table*) It doesn't matter. I'm an easy crier.
LEE	So, why didn't you tell me?

MARY   You didn't give me a chance! You just said "I'm
         dying" out of nowhere. I didn't see it coming. You
         should've built up to it.

LEE   Built up to it?

MARY   Yes. Tell me you're not feeling well, and work up
         from there. (*starts to eat the cake, in her despair*)

LEE   All right, I'm sorry. I had no idea it would affect
         you like this.

MARY   (*crying and eating*) Oh, it's not just you. It's
         everything. I mean, here you are... you seem
         like a nice guy. You've got a wife. You've probably
         got kids.

LEE   Two girls.

MARY   (*moaning through her mouthful of cake*) Oh, there you
         go, you've got a family. And what happens? You're
         dying. And then, here I am... I'm a good person,
         right? Things seem to be going along fine. I'm
         happy. Then bingo! Just like that, my husband
         skips town...

         *LORETTA enters left. Her hair is damp, and she is
         carrying her shoes.*

LORETTA Oh, that was just what I needed. I've got my second
         wind now. I feel like dancing some more. (*dances a
         couple of steps*) What do you think? Let's put some
         music on. (*dances some more*) Huh? Little music?
         (*notices that LEE and MARY don't seem too chipper and
         she stops dancing*) What's the matter? (*looks at LEE,
         then MARY*) Mary?

MARY   Nothing's the matter.

LORETTA Mary, your eyes are all red. Have you been crying?
         (*sits at the table*)

         LEE moves right and sits in the rocking chair.

MARY   No.

LORETTA   Aw, did you two have a fight?

MARY   Oh, don't be ridiculous.

LORETTA   Well, what is it then? (*bends to put her shoes on*)

MARY   (*through a mouthful of cake*) He's dying.

LORETTA   (*didn't hear MARY*) What?

MARY   He's dying.

LORETTA   I can't hear you.

MARY   Oh, for Godsake, Loretta!

LORETTA   Well, speak up.

MARY   (*loudly*) I said he's dying!

LORETTA   That's better. (*beat*) Who's dying?

MARY   (*pointing to LEE*) Him.

> *LORETTA looks at LEE. LEE raises his hand, as if volunteering.*

LORETTA   What'd you do? Eat some of the cake?

MARY   Loretta!

LORETTA   Well, what to you mean, he's dying?

MARY   I mean, he's dying. He just told me.

LORETTA   He told you that?

MARY   Yes.

LORETTA   (*standing and approaching LEE*) Uh-huh. And I suppose you want Mary to fulfill a dying man's wish. Is that it?

MARY   Loretta, it's not like that.

LORETTA   Oh, really, Mary. Wake up! It's a come-on. (*to LEE*) Is this the way you guys get girls where you come from? I mean, I'd expect this sort of thing from your brother, but not from you. (*moves right to LEE*)

LEE   Where is Owen, anyway?

LORETTA   He's looking for his pants. Now, don't change the subject. I want to hear some more about this dying business.

MARY   (*moving right, in front of the couch*) Loretta, please. You're making a fool of yourself.

LORETTA   Well, all right, so what's he dying of?

MARY   I don't know. We didn't get that far. (*sits on the couch*)

LEE   If you want the medical term, it's called malignant melanoma.

LORETTA   Melanoma? Oh, he's done his homework. And I suppose you're going to tell us you've got about what, six months to live?

LEE   No, probably closer to a year.

LORETTA   Oh, it's a year, is it? Good.

LEE   Well, depending on how the treatment goes, yeah.

LORETTA   Uh-huh. (*starts to feel uneasy*) Okay, enough's enough. Mary, tell him to knock it off. He's going to spoil the whole night.

LEE   Look, I'm sorry. (*gets up*) I really had no right to bring this up with strangers. Let's just drop it, okay? (*moves upstage; and exits to the bathroom*)

LORETTA   So, is he putting us on, or what?

MARY   No, he's telling the truth. I'm sure of it.

LORETTA   (*sits beside MARY to comfort her*) Oh, Mary. Oh, you poor kid. I mean, it's bad enough that he's married, but, dying too? I guess this just isn't your day.

> *LEE enters from the bathroom, carrying a towel. He hands it to LORETTA.*

LEE   Here.

LORETTA   Thanks. (*takes towel and mops her hair*)

> *LEE goes about picking up the beer cans that have accumulated during the day, and putting them in the trash can upstage left. LORETTA moves upstage to the kitchen area.*

So... how does it feel to know you're going to die?

LEE   Well, we all know we're going to die sometime.

LORETTA   Yeah, but while the rest of us are still worrying about it, you're going to be dead.

MARY   (*slumping back in the couch*) Oh, God.

LORETTA   (*to MARY*) Well, I don't know what to say. What do you say to a guy who's dying?

LEE   Hey, don't worry about it. You're doing just fine. I'll tell you what it's like. It's like I'm at the movies, and I'm in the front row, and then... the movie ends, and I'm staring up at this white screen. It's like everything that's going to happen has happened, and now I'm just staring at white.

MARY   (*moves upstage, to the bathroom*) Would you excuse me, please? (*near tears again, she exits to the bathroom*)

LORETTA   As you can see, my sister's the sensitive type.

LEE   Uh-huh. But, you're not, is that right?

LORETTA   Well, I try and avoid it whenever I can. (*moves downstage centre to the couch*) So, what are you going to do now? I mean, now that you know you've only got a year left. (*sits on the couch*)

LEE   Well, we'll probably travel a bit. Arlene, that's my wife, she's always wanted to do some travelling. (*sits on the couch*)

LORETTA   Is she dying too?

LEE   No.

LORETTA   Then don't do what she wants to do. What do you want to do?

LEE   Well, not a whole lot really.

LORETTA   Oh, come on. There must be something. Everybody's got at least one thing they've always dreamed of doing. Don't you have any dreams like that?

LEE   Sure, I have dreams.

LORETTA   Well, what are they?

LEE   (*beat*) No, it's stupid. It's out of reach now.

LORETTA   Well, of course it's out of reach. It wouldn't be a dream if it wasn't out of reach. What is it?

LEE   (*almost embarrassed to tell her*) Well, I always thought I might play professional football one day. At least, when I was playing high school ball, I used to think that. I used to imagine myself playing in one of those big stadiums, in front of all those fans... I was pretty good in high school. Just needed a little more weight, they said. I'm sure I could've made it in the college ranks, but I never got that far. (*beat*) Boy, it didn't seem out of reach back then. Nothing... nothing seemed out of reach back then. I knew exactly what I was going to do. I was going to give football a shot, and if that didn't work out, then I was going to open my own sporting goods store.

LORETTA   So, what happened?

LEE   Uh, well, my Dad got sick and I had to go on full-time at the plant.

LORETTA   Oh. And you're sure about this? About dying? I mean, they couldn't have made a mistake, could they?

LEE   Oh, no. There's no mistake. Believe me, I made sure they double checked.

> *MARY enters from the bathroom. She moves downstage to the rocking chair.*

MARY   I... uh, I'm sorry. I was just feeling a little down. I won't let it happen again. (*sits in the rocker*)

LEE   Listen, I didn't mean for things to turn out this way. This is exactly what I didn't want.

LORETTA   You know what I'd do if I found out I only had a year to live?

MARY   Oh, do you have to keep talking about this?

LORETTA   (*standing*) No, listen to me now. I'd throw myself a party. (*moves around behind the couch*) No.... No, a whole lot of parties, so it would seem like one big party that lasted the whole year. Don't you think a person should go out like that?

MARY   No, I don't.

LORETTA   Well, all right then, what would you do if you were going to die in a year?

MARY   I think, Loretta, that I would figure out a way to take you with me.

> *OWEN enters, left. He carries his shoes, and his pants are wet below the knees.*

OWEN   I found them. They got caught up in the bushes down by the shore. So, how are we doing in here? Still going strong?

LEE   Actually, things were just starting to wind down.

OWEN   Well, we'll just have to wind them back up again.
               (*moves upstage to the fridge to get a beer*)

LORETTA   (*moving to OWEN*) Let me ask you something. Don't
               you think that if a person's going to die, they should
               die happy? Like at a party, surrounded by friends?

OWEN   (*uneasy, but tries to smile about it*) What? What the hell
               kind of question is that? What've you people been
               doing in here, anyway?

LORETTA   We're having an argument about what a person
               would do if they knew they only had so much time
               left.

MARY   Loretta, I think we should drop it.

LORETTA   No. (*to OWEN*) Now, come on. What would you do?

OWEN   (*moving downstage, slowly*) What do you mean, what
               would I do? Do about what?

LORETTA   (*following him*) If you only had a year left. What
               would you do?

OWEN   How should I know? I never thought about it.

LORETTA   Oh, you must have thought about it. Come on.

OWEN   (*moving right*) I'd better change these pants. They're
               kind of damp.

LORETTA   (*moves after OWEN, and stops him*) Oh, no you don't.
               You're not getting off that easily.

MARY   Loretta...

LORETTA   You've got to help us settle this. Now, what would
               you do?

OWEN   I don't know.

LORETTA Well, think.

OWEN (*suddenly angry*) I said, I don't know! All right? (*turns and moves to the bedroom, right*) I've gotta change. (*exits to the bedroom*)

LORETTA Well, what the hell's wrong with him?

LEE It's okay. He's just having a hard time accepting things. (*gets up and moves to the bedroom door*)

MARY (*to LORETTA*) Are you satisfied now?

LEE (*knocking on the bedroom door*) Owen?

LORETTA Wait a minute. I'll go. (*moves upstage to the refrigerator; takes out a six pack of beer*)

MARY I think you've done enough already.

LORETTA No, no, never let it be said that I didn't clean up my own mess. (*moving to the bedroom*)

LEE What are you going to do?

LORETTA I'm going to cheer him up.

LEE Now, hold on, now. I think you should know that Owen is engaged to be married in three weeks.

LORETTA What? He didn't tell me that. (*moving to the bedroom*) Owen, congratulations! I just heard! (*exits to the bedroom*)

LEE (*to MARY*) Are you sure you two are sisters?

MARY I'm sorry about her.

LEE No, it's not her fault. It's Owen. He's being unreasonable.

MARY Well, what do you expect?

LEE   I expect him to stop ignoring the situation. To stop
        acting as if the problem isn't there. All he wants to
        do is chase women and fish. Fish, for Godsake! We
        haven't fished in ten years. Not since Dad died.
        I can't understand what he's thinking.

MARY   I can. He just wants things to be the way they used
        to be.

LEE   Yeah, don't we all.

MARY   Well, can't you give him that? Just for one weekend?

LEE   No.

MARY   Why?

LEE   Because it can't be the way it used to be. It never
        will be again. If anybody should know that, you
        should. Can't you see? You sit around hoping for
        things that you can't have, trying to grab on to some
        ghost that was part of your life, God knows when,
        and you wind up with nothing!

MARY   (*rising*) Oh, is that right?

LEE   That's right.

MARY   Well, let me tell you something, mister. Don't start
        preaching to me about how things can't be the way
        they used to be, because I, for one, am counting on
        it. And if I want to sit around for two years, or five
        years, or ten years and wait for some clown to come
        home with my car, then I'll goddamn wait! And if,
        for some reason, I get it in my mind that I want to go
        out on a date, then I'll go out. And don't you tell me
        this isn't a date. Don't you dare. Your brother stood
        right here and asked us if we'd go with you, and we
        said yes.

LEE   Now, that was Owen's idea. Not mine.

MARY   I don't care whose idea it was. We went! We had
        dinner with you. We danced with you. We put

dresses on. How many women did you see there
tonight with dresses on? Three! Me, Loretta, and
Mrs. Gunther, who's a cow and can't fit into a pair of
pants anyway. So, don't tell me this isn't a date. I
haven't been out with a man in two years, and I
don't appreciate the fact that the first time I do go
out, it gets passed off as a car pool. It's a date! And
it's not over yet. So, you'd better start showing me a
good time, and pretty goddamn fast!

> *MARY stands there, shocked at herself slightly for
> yelling at LEE. LEE moves to her. He takes her by the
> arms and moves in slowly, to kiss her. Then he changes
> his mind.*

LEE   Uh.... You want to play some cards?

MARY   Cards?... Sure... cards'll be fine.

LEE   Good. I'll get them then.

MARY   Good.

> *LEE moves upstage to the cupboards and finds a deck
> of cards. Then he moves downstage by the screen door
> and stands there shuffling them. Still standing where
> LEE left her, MARY gives a nervous laugh.*

I guess I lost my temper there. I don't do that very
often. I can usually keep it under control. As a
matter of fact, that used to drive my husband crazy.
He'd get mad at something, and I'd stay calm. And
the calmer I stayed... the madder he got. (*beat, doesn't
know whether to laugh or cry*) Maybe I should've got
mad more often.

LEE   So, uh, what do you want to play?

MARY   (*moving upstage to the sink*) Oh, it doesn't matter.
            Whatever you want. (*finds a cloth and goes to wipe off
            the table*)

LEE   How about poker?

MARY That's fine.

LEE Okay, five card stud. No draw. Nothing wild. (*stands at the table and deals the first hand around MARY's wiping*)

MARY (*after a short pause*) You were going to kiss me, weren't you?

LEE Yeah, for a minute there, it sure looked like it.

MARY So, why didn't you?

LEE I don't know.

MARY Was it because we're both married? Was that it?

LEE Probably.

MARY Yeah, I guess you didn't think it would be proper.

LEE Right.

MARY Yeah, that's what I figured. (*puts the cloth back in the sink*)

> LEE sits, and MARY returns to the table and sits. They look at their cards.

LEE All set?

MARY (*looking at her cards*) I guess so.

LEE What've you got?

MARY Two pair.

LEE (*throwing his cards in*) Beats me. Your deal.

MARY (*shuffling and dealing*) Do you think it's stupid... the fact that I still consider myself married?

LEE Sure I do.

MARY	Well, I don't think it's stupid. I mean, I am still married.
LEE	Oh, I know you are.
MARY	I'll admit that, sometimes, I don't feel married.
LEE	Yeah, hard to feel married with no husband and no car.
MARY	But, it is legal. The marriage is still in effect as far as the courts are concerned, so I should consider myself married.
LEE	That's right. You don't want to go breaking any laws. A pair of kings.
MARY	Three threes. I win again. (*lays her hand down*)
LEE	So you do.

> LEE *throws his hand down rather vigorously. He's a little annoyed at losing. He picks up the cards and starts to shuffle.*

	So, are you having fun now?
MARY	Oh, yeah.
LEE	Good.
MARY	How about you?
LEE	(*nodding*) Well...
MARY	(*almost teasing*) Oh, come on, now. You're having fun. Admit it.
LEE	(*smiling*) Yeah, I'm having fun.
MARY	Good. (*picks up her cards*) Do you still want to kiss me?
LEE	(*looks at her for a moment*) Naw. (*looks back at his cards*)

MARY   It's just that I thought that, you know, a man who's faced with the situation you're faced with... well, I thought he might just throw caution to the wind.

LEE   Yeah, I can see your point.

MARY   And you don't feel that way?

LEE   Not yet.

MARY   Oh.

LEE   Maybe when I get a little further along, I'll start to get more adventurous. What've you got?

MARY   Full house.

LEE   (*throws his cards down vigorously again*) Your deal.

MARY   (*shuffling and dealing*) So, do you play poker a lot?

LEE   Once in a while.

MARY   You know, we can play something else if you like.

LEE   No, no. This is fine. I'm not nearly as good at other games.

MARY   (*after a short pause*) Listen, would you do me a favour?

LEE   Sure. What?

MARY   When you get a little further along, and you start to get more adventurous... would you call me?

LEE   (*beat*) Yeah, I'll do that.

MARY   Good. Oh, look at that. Straight flush. (*laughs*) Looks like you're in for a long night.

LEE   (*good naturedly*) You know what you are?

MARY   What?

LEE   You're ruthless. I mean, show me some mercy here. This could be the last card game I ever play.

MARY   (*smiling*) Shut up and deal.

     Lights down.

ACT TWO

SCENE 1

*The next morning. The cabin. As the scene opens,
MARY is sitting in the porch. She is wearing Aunt
Rose's sweater coat, and she's drinking a cup of coffee.
The bedroom door opens. OWEN enters looking
horribly hung-over. He closes the door softly behind
him and makes his way up to the bathroom. He enters
the bathroom and closes the door. He's only in there for
about ten or fifteen seconds, and when he enters the
living area again, he smacks his lips as though his
mouth feels a whole lot fresher. He moves left and
notices MARY, who is now standing, watching him
through the screen door.*

OWEN   Morning.

MARY   Good morning.

OWEN   Any coffee?

MARY   On the stove.

*OWEN goes upstage and gets a cup from the
cupboard. MARY steps inside. OWEN moves to
the stove, then turns back and goes to the refrigerator.
He takes out a beer, pops it open, and pours some into
the cup.*

Feeling a little ragged this morning, are we?

OWEN   Huh? Oh, yeah, well, it was kind of a rough night.
How 'bout you? How are you feeling?

MARY   Oh, I'm fine. A little tired. I didn't get much sleep.

OWEN   *(with a dirty laugh)* Yeah, I know what you mean. *(sits
at the table)*

MARY   *(not amused)* What's Loretta doing? Is she getting up
soon?

OWEN	Well, I don't know. She didn't get much sleep last night either.
MARY	(*moving right*) You don't say.
OWEN	Yeah. Course, I suppose that's my fault.
MARY	(*turning on him*) Look, I don't mind you sleeping with my sister. That's her business. But, please don't come strutting around me like some neanderthal who's just bagged the season's first giant sloth! (*takes off the sweater and hangs it up, upstage right*)
OWEN	Hey, sorry. I was just making conversation. (*beat*) What were you doing out there?
MARY	Watching your brother. He went out in the boat about an hour ago.
OWEN	(*getting up and moving to the screen door*) Oh, yeah? What's he doing? Fishing?
MARY	No, just sitting.
OWEN	Well, if that was me out there, I'd be fishing. But, Lee, he's always been a thinker.
MARY	Yeah, he's a good guy.
OWEN	Well, he's my brother.
MARY	Owen... could you keep an eye on him for the next little while? Just to make sure that nothing happens to him.
OWEN	Like what?
MARY	I don't know. Anything. Things happen to people.
OWEN	Listen don't worry about Lee. He can look after himself. (*moves back to the table and sits*)
MARY	No, that's not what I mean. (*moves to the table and sits*) What I'm saying is, that a man in his condition...

he, uh... he might decide to... well, he might not want to carry things through to their natural end. He might decide to hurry it along in some way.

OWEN   Hurry it along?

MARY   Yeah . You know, give it a little nudge .

OWEN   A nudge? You mean, you think.... You think that Lee.... Did he tell you he was going to do something?

MARY   No, not exactly...

OWEN   Not exactly? Well, what exactly did he say?

MARY   He just said that the idea had crossed his mind once or twice.

OWEN   I don't believe that.

MARY   Owen, why would I lie?

OWEN   He's never said anything like that to me. Why would he tell you? No, no way. (*gets up and moves left*) Lee's not going to hurry anything along. Not like that.

MARY   Yes, but it couldn't hurt to watch him. Just to be safe. I mean, some people do strange things when they're under stress.

OWEN   Not Lee! No sir. He's as steady as they come. Take it from me. He's my brother, for Godsake! I know him better than anyone. And there's no way he'd do that.

MARY   Are you sure?

> OWEN *pauses for a moment and looks at MARY, then out the screen door, then back to MARY. Then he rushes into the porch.*

OWEN   Lee, you get the hell in here right now! Lee? Did you hear me? I want you in here, and I want you in here now!

The bedroom door opens and LORETTA enters, looking every bit as bad as OWEN did. Her hair is tousled and she has one shoe on and the other in her hand.

LORETTA   Quiet!!

LORETTA pauses. She gets her breath, and looks at MARY. She speaks as if still half asleep.

Mary. You still here? That's nice. (*moves upstage to the bathroom*)

OWEN   (*enters from the porch*) Good morning.

LORETTA gives a pathetic wave without looking, and exits to the bathroom.

(*to MARY*) Uh, listen, Mary, I have to talk to your sister alone for a minute. Do you mind?

MARY   What about Lee?

OWEN   Yeah, well, I wouldn't ask, but it's very important. I mean, if I don't talk to her now, I might not get another chance. Maybe you could go down to the shore there and make sure Lee gets in all right. Would you do that for me? (*yelling out the door*) Lee, I'm giving you five minutes to get the hell in here! (*to MARY*) Please, Mary?

MARY moves to the screen door, and exits left.

Oh, thanks. I appreciate it. (*yelling*) Lee? Four and a half minutes! (*to MARY*) Thanks again, Mary.

LORETTA enters from the bathroom.

LORETTA   Is that coffee I smell?

OWEN   Yeah, we've got a whole pot here.

LORETTA   Could you pour me a cup, please? (*moves slowly to the kitchen area*)

OWEN   Sure. (*gets her a cup and moves to pour her coffee*)

LORETTA   Oh, I must look awful.

            LORETTA waits for OWEN to contradict her.

            Well?

OWEN   Hmm? What?

LORETTA   Well, how do I look?

OWEN   Oh, terrific. Really terrific.

LORETTA   You're just saying that, aren't you?

OWEN   No, I mean it. Really. You look great. You look
            beautiful.

LORETTA   Okay, don't overdo it. (*turns to the refrigerator*)

OWEN   (*turns to the stove to pour LORETTA's coffee*) How do
            you take your coffee?

LORETTA   Just black. (*opens the fridge and sticks her head in the
            freezer*)

OWEN   Okay, here you go.

            *OWEN moves downstage to the table with
            LORETTA's cup of coffee. He sets it on the table for
            her. Then he turns and sees LORETTA in the freezer.
            He moves upstage slowly. He leans on the refrigerator.
            He motions as if he's going to knock lightly on the top
            of the refrigerator to get her attention, but then he
            stops.*

            Loretta?... What are you doing?

LORETTA   I'm exposing my face to the cold.

OWEN   What for?

LORETTA   To tighten my skin up.

OWEN   (*beat*) Why?

LORETTA   So I won't have wrinkles when I'm older.

OWEN   Oh. Does it work?

LORETTA   (*removing her head slowly from the freezer and looking at OWEN*) Well, we won't know until I'm older, now will we? (*sticks her head back in the freezer*)

OWEN   Listen, Loretta, I have to talk to you about something.

LORETTA   Go ahead.

OWEN   No, I can't talk to you when you've got your head in the freezer. Could you come out of there, please? (*moves downstage to the screen door*) Lee! You've got three minutes! (*to LORETTA*) Loretta, please, this is very important.

LORETTA   Oh, all right.

> *LORETTA closes the refrigerator, and moves downstage to the table. She sits, and slaps her face a couple of times.*

OWEN   Thank you. (*out the door*) Mary, you tell him he's got three minutes, and then I'm calling the coast guard.

LORETTA   We don't have a coast guard. This is a lake. We don't even have a coast. (*sips her coffee*)

OWEN   I don't know what I'm worried about. He's not going to do anything.

LORETTA   Mmmm, that's good. You know, I think I should do coffee commercials. I wonder what I'd look like in a kitchen.

OWEN   (*moving to the table*) Okay, now listen to me, Loretta. I don't want you to miss what I'm saying here.

LORETTA   I'm listening. What's the problem?

OWEN   (*sits at the table*) Well, the thing is, I'm engaged to be married in three weeks.

LORETTA   Yeah, I know that.

OWEN   I know you know.

LORETTA   Well, what are you telling me something I already know for?

OWEN   That wasn't what I wanted to tell you. I was just leading into it. Now, please, don't interrupt me. I've got all this laid out in my head, and if you interrupt me, I'll lose my place. Now, I'm getting married in three weeks. The invitations have gone out. We've been measured for the suits. Everything's set to go. Except... and here's the problem... Patty and I aren't right for each other. It's all wrong. I can see that now. I was thinking about it last night, after you fell asleep, and I said to myself, "Is Patty the girl that you want to spend the rest of your life with?" And I thought about that.... The rest of my life. Well, that's when it hit me. I mean, the answer is no. She's not the girl. Oh, she's nice enough, sure. But, not for the rest of my life. No, I realise that now. And it's because of you. Yeah, because last night... last night, I had more fun with you than I've ever had with Patty. Ever.

LORETTA   Well, I'll admit, I was cooking.

OWEN   Now, I want you to listen carefully to this next part because it might come as a bit of a surprise to you. So, pay attention, and listen to what I'm saying. (*beat*) I like you. I like you a lot. And I've got a real good job down at the plant. A real secure job. I mean, I'm making more money right now than my Dad ever made, and he was foreman. And I'm thinking of going back to school too.... Night school, so I'll have something to fall back on just in case. Now, keeping all that in mind, I was wondering if maybe you would... well, if maybe you and I could start seeing each other on a regular basis... with the thought that somewhere down the road, maybe in a

year or so, if everything goes all right... maybe
we could make it more regular. Maybe even...
permanent. Do you understand what I'm saying
so far?

LORETTA   (*beat*) Are you asking me to marry you?

OWEN   No, not outright. No. I'm just asking you to go out
            with me for a while with the option of marrying me
            later on. And I don't want to rush you, but I have to
            know today.

LORETTA   Are you serious?

OWEN   Well, I know it's kind of short notice, but I think I
            should call the wedding off, and I don't want to
            leave it 'til the last minute.

LORETTA   You're out of your mind.

OWEN   Did you want some time to think about it?

LORETTA   (*starting to laugh*) You're out of your goddamn mind.

OWEN   You're surprised, aren't you?

LORETTA   Oh, you got that right.

OWEN   (*laughing along*) Yeah, I figured you would be. (*the
            laughter dies down*) So, what do you think?

LORETTA   Oh, come on, Owen. What do you mean, what do I
            think? I think we both probably had a little too much
            to drink last night, and things looked a bit more
            promising to you than they actually were .

OWEN   Didn't you have a good time last night?

LORETTA   Sure I had a good time. So what? You want me to
            marry you because I had a good time?

OWEN   Now, I didn't ask you to marry me.

LORETTA   Oh, right. Yeah, you want me to go out with you for a while, with the option of marrying you later on. And why? Because you've got a secure job, and you can keep me in flower pots for the rest of my life! Well, I'm sorry, but that's not reason enough for me.

OWEN   You don't like where I work, is that it?

LORETTA   I don't care where you work, Owen. That's got nothing to do with it.

OWEN   I told you I was thinking of going back to school. Hey, pretty soon there's going to be a lot of opportunities coming my way.

LORETTA   (*becoming more forceful*) No, you're not listening to me. Listen to me! Stop trying to barge your way into my life. I've got plans. I've got a future. I've been on television! Don't you know what that means? I can't get married right now. Not to you. Not to anybody.

OWEN   I just want to be with you. I can talk to you. I've never really talked to a girl before. I've never met anyone like you.

LORETTA   How can you say that? How can you be so sure?

OWEN   But, I am.

LORETTA   Owen, we have known each other for one day. One day! My God, it takes me that long to pick out a pair of shoes. No. No, you just go back home to... to.... (*starts to laugh*) Oh, God, this is funny. Don't you see how funny this is? I don't even know where you live. I don't even know your last name. You don't know my real last name. Don't you think that's funny? Boy, I sure as hell do. No, I'll tell you what you do. You go back home, and we'll just say this never happened. (*moves to the screen door and yells out*) Mary, can we get going please?

OWEN   Is that what you're going to do? Just forget about it?

LORETTA   Well... I suppose not. Not for a long while anyway. Look, Owen, I know you're going through a rough time right now, but I'm not the answer. I'm not going to make it all better.

OWEN   (*quietly*) I wish you'd think it over. I mean, I don't have to know today.

LORETTA   (*smiling, feeling sorry for him*) You really are something, you know that?

      MARY enters, left.

Come on, Mary. Let's go. (*moves to get her life jacket*)

MARY   What's the hurry?

LORETTA   No hurry. I'm just ready to go, that's all. (*puts her life jacket on*)

MARY   But I didn't get a chance to say good-bye.

LORETTA   Oh, come on. He might stay out there for hours yet.

MARY   So what? Why do we have to rush off all of a sudden?

LORETTA   We have been here all night, Mary. I would hardly call it rushing off.

MARY   Well, we have been here all night because of you, Miss twenty-four hour convenience. (*moves right*) Well, now it's my turn. Maybe I feel like staying around for a while.

LORETTA   (*pleading*) Mary, please. I'll explain later. Now, hurry up.

      LORETTA moves into the porch. MARY moves reluctantly to get her life jacket and purse.

MARY   (*to OWEN*) He's not out there anymore. He moved off down the lake. Are you going to do what I said, or am I going to have to follow you home and do it myself?

OWEN   No, no. I'll do it.

MARY   Promise?

OWEN   Yeah, but I still say there's no reason to.

MARY   Well, just do it anyway, okay? For me.

OWEN   Yeah.

MARY   (*starts to pick up the cake container, and then sets it down again*) Here's a gift. (*moves left toward the screen door*) Will you say good-bye to him for me?

OWEN   Uh-huh.

MARY   Thanks. And tell him I had a good time last night, and I... well, just tell him I had a good time, and it was nice meeting him and all that.

OWEN   Sure.

MARY   (*starts to leave, then stops*) And tell him.... Tell him I've decided to buy a new car. Will you do that?

OWEN   New car?

MARY   He'll know what I mean.

OWEN   Whatever you say.

MARY   Thanks. (*turns to leave*)

OWEN   Listen... uh, if we come up again next year, maybe the four of us can get together again. Go to another dance.

MARY   (*hesitant*) Yeah, you never know. Maybe we will.

LORETTA   (*from the porch*) Mary.

MARY   All right, I'm coming. (*to OWEN*) Well, take care of yourself.

OWEN   You too.

> *MARY exits left. LORETTA steps back inside and gives OWEN a kiss.*

LORETTA   Good-bye.

OWEN   Bye.

LORETTA   And stop looking so goddamn miserable, will ya? (*turns to leave*)

OWEN   Hey.

LORETTA   (*turning back*) What?

OWEN   It's no big deal, you know. I mean, that you said no. I kind of expected you to say no anyway, so, it's no big thing. You're not mad are you?

LORETTA   No, I'm not mad.

OWEN   Good.

LORETTA   It was pretty dumb though, you must admit.

> *LORETTA gives a little laugh. OWEN doesn't laugh. He just looks.*

OWEN   Yeah. Anyway, good luck with your career. I hope everything works out for you, you know. I really hope you do well. I hope you get what you want.

LORETTA   Thanks.

OWEN   And I hope... well, I just hope you do well, that's all.

LORETTA   Yeah. Well, good-bye. (*exits left*)

> *OWEN watches her until she is well out of sight.*

OWEN   (*to himself*) I hope your boat sinks.

> *Lights down.*

SCENE 2

About two hours later. The cabin. OWEN is sitting in the rocking chair, right, with a can of beer in his hand. There are five or six empty beer cans on the table. OWEN is looking very serious as LEE enters through the screen door, left.

LEE   Hi. (*moves upstage to the kitchen area, to pour himself a coffee*) It's a beautiful day out there. Gonna be a real hot one I think. Maybe we can go for a swim before we leave, huh? Probably the last chance we'll get this year. Uh... sorry I was gone so long. I'd forgotten how big this lake was. I was just going to do a little exploring, and I guess I got carried away. I wound up way the hell down by the old train bridge. Hey, remember the day Dad dove off that thing. Scared me half to death. (*picks up one of the empty beer cans*) I see you've had your breakfast. Good. Most important meal of the day, they say. (*puts the can down and moves to the screen door*) So, how long ago did the girls leave?

OWEN   Couple of hours.

LEE   That's too bad. I didn't get a chance to say good-bye. I didn't think they'd be leaving that soon. Did they say anything?

OWEN   Like what?

LEE   Well, I don't know. Like about last night, or anything?

OWEN   No, not really. Just said good-bye and left.

LEE   Uh-huh. Well, maybe we can stop in and see them at the store on the way out. (*beat*) Listen, Owen, I was hoping that you and I would get a chance to talk this weekend but, the way it turned out, with the girls here and all, we never got any time alone...

OWEN   Well, now, that's strange, because I've been sitting here alone for two hours. I've had plenty of time to talk. Just didn't have anyone to talk to.

LEE   I said I was sorry...

OWEN   I did think of going fishing, but then, I didn't have a boat.

LEE   All right, I'm sorry. I'm sorry I spoiled your day.

OWEN   (*gets up and moves to the kitchen area*) Spoiled my day? Hell, you didn't spoil my day. The best is still to come. We haven't been to the dump yet. (*sets his empty beer can on the table, and goes to the fridge to get another*)

LEE   Okay, Owen, what is it? What's the matter?

OWEN   Not a thing.

LEE   Oh, I know what it is. You're feeling guilty, right? And you're taking it out on me.

OWEN   Guilty?

LEE   (*moving to OWEN*) Yes. About fooling around with Loretta when you're getting married in three weeks. Well, I don't blame you. You should feel guilty.

OWEN   (*moving downstage right*) Oh is that right? Well, it shows how much you know, Mr. Grade Ten graduate. Number one; I don't feel guilty. And Number Two; I'm not getting married in three weeks. (*sits in the rocker*)

LEE   What?

OWEN   That's right. My nuptials have been postponed indefinitely. I am no longer betrothed. I am unbetrothed. De-betrothed. Without betrothment. So, what do you think of that?

LEE   I think you're drunk.

OWEN   Wrong again, professor.

LEE   (*moving downstage in front of the couch*) All right,
       do you mind telling me why you're not getting
       married? (*sits on the couch*)

OWEN   Well, why should I get married? I'm still young.
       I don't want to get tied down to one woman already.
       I mean, I've got it made now. I'm moving up. Yeah,
       I'm gonna have a better paying job. Why should I
       settle for Patty? I think I'll just play the field for a
       while. See what else I can scare up.

LEE   I don't understand. What better paying job?

OWEN   (*beat*) Well, yours. I mean, I'm gonna get your job,
       right? They're gonna want to keep it in the Melville
       family, aren't they? Sure. Dad dies, and you become
       foreman. You die, and I become foreman. That's the
       way it works, isn't it? And then when I die... Mom
       gets to be foreman! God, we've got our own little
       plastic dynasty here.

       LEE gets up and moves away, left.

       And you want to talk about guilt. I think you're the
       one who's feeling guilty.

LEE   Me? What have I got to feel guilty about?

OWEN   (*standing and moving to LEE*) Oh, come on. You and
       Mary? Out here last night?

LEE   We didn't do anything! We played cards all night.

OWEN   Cards?

LEE   Yeah, cards.

OWEN   You mean to tell me that you spent the whole night
       out here, with the loneliest woman on the lake, and
       all you did was play cards?

LEE   No, that's not all we did.

OWEN   Ah-hah!

LEE	No, we laughed a lot too. And we talked a lot. And we listened. All the things my own family won't even do. And I loved every minute of it. (*beat*) I'm going to get some breakfast. You'd better get packed. (*moves upstage to the refrigerator to take out the eggs*)
OWEN	(*following LEE*) Oh, all right. Hey, you wanna talk? Terrific. Let's talk.
LEE	Some other time, Owen. When you've had a little less to drink.
OWEN	(*taking the eggs from LEE, and putting them back in the refrigerator*) No, we'll talk right now. Right here. (*moving downstage left*) Now, let me see, what will we talk about? Oh, I know. Let's start with what the hell you've been doing out there all morning.
LEE	I told you. I went for a boat ride.
OWEN	And what else?
LEE	Nothing else! What else do you do on a boat ride? You sit in the damn boat, and you ride.
OWEN	And you didn't do any thinking while you were out there?
LEE	Any what?
OWEN	Thinking. You know, with your head? I mean, you must have been thinking about something.
LEE	I was thinking about a lot of things. I've got a lot on my mind!
OWEN	Ahhh, now we're getting warmer. Now we're on the right track. And what would these things be that you have on your mind? What kind of things? Would you like me to guess?
LEE	I'm not going to talk to you when you're like this, Owen. You're not making sense. (*goes to fridge, and takes out the eggs; moves to the counter upstage centre and takes down a bowl*)

OWEN   Oh, I'm sorry. That must be my lack of schooling.
            Now, Mary... there's a girl who makes sense. Yeah,
            she was telling me this morning about the things
            people do when they're under stress. Well, like you.
            You're under stress, right? And she was saying that a
            lot of people like you would just say, "The hell with
            it. Let's get it over with." Is that what you were
            thinking about out there?

LEE   What are you getting at?

OWEN   Oh, come on, Lee. I know about this alternative of
            yours. Mary told me all about it. Yeah, she asked
            me to keep an eye on you, to make sure nothing
            happened to you. That was thoughtful of her,
            wasn't it?

LEE   That was between Mary and me. She shouldn't have
            told you.

OWEN   (*angry*) You're damn right she shouldn't have. You
            should've told me, Lee! You! How do you think
            I feel hearing that from someone I hardly know?

LEE   When would you ever give me a chance to tell you?
            Huh? When?

OWEN   You've had plenty of chances.

LEE   I've had nothing! I've had nothing from you or
            anybody else in the family. You're gonna have to
            face this thing sooner or later, Owen. It might as
            well be now.

OWEN   (*beat*) All right. (*picks up the gun, puts a bullet in it,
            and lays it on the table*) All right, let's face it now
            then. There you are. Go ahead.

LEE   What's that supposed to be?

OWEN   Go ahead. You want to do it now? Go on.

LEE   Owen, I said I'd thought about it. It's only natural.
            I didn't say I was going to do it.

OWEN   No, go on. Pick it up.

LEE   You're out of your mind.

OWEN   I said pick it up!! You're so anxious. Come on!

LEE   No!

OWEN   Pick it up, damn it! Pick it up!

LEE   (*angry*) I'm warning you, Owen! You cool off! Now, I'm gonna make some breakfast, you're gonna get packed, and we're gonna forget about this whole goddamn thing!

OWEN   I'll tell you what we're gonna forget about. We're gonna forget about your breakfast, that's what we're gonna forget about. (*knocks the eggs and frying pan onto the floor*) Now, are you gonna pick up the gun, or am I? Huh? Or is that what you want? Should I do it for you? I will if you want.

LEE   Okay, go ahead. Go on, do it.

OWEN   I will, Lee. I swear, I will.

LEE   Fine. Come on.

        OWEN doesn't move.

        Come on! At last you can do something to help me. (*picks up the gun*) Here! Take it!

OWEN   Don't kid around, Lee.

LEE   Who's kidding? This way, I won't have to worry about when it's going to happen. Next week. A month from now. Two months. Come on. (*pushes the gun at OWEN*) Right now.

OWEN   (*scared*) Cut it out.

LEE   No! You wanna do it? Come on! (*turns the gun around, pointing the safe end at OWEN*) You'll be doing me a favour. Now I won't have to say good-bye to everybody. Oh, I was going to hate that part. But, now, you can do it for me. You will, won't you? You'll say good-bye to everybody?

LEE backs OWEN up.

OWEN   (*almost in tears*) No.

LEE   Sure! You can do that much for me, can't you? I mean, what's a brother for?'

OWEN   (*in tears*) No! (*grabs LEE, and hugs him*) Goddamn it, Lee! Goddamn it, why do you have to die?

LEE   (*compassionately*) Owen... Owen, it's all right.

OWEN breaks away and wipes his eyes.

OWEN   I've always had you around, Lee. I don't know what it's like not having you around... telling me what to do. You and Dad always did that for me. I could always count on that. And even after Dad died... it wasn't so bad, because you were still there, still telling me what to do. You should've let me grow up, Lee. You should've let me grow up on my own.

LEE   I tried...

OWEN   (*angry*) You tried. You tried too late! You didn't start trying until after you found out you were going to die. That's when you started trying. That's what all this going back to school business is about. And learning myself a trade. You're just as scared as I am. You think I'm gonna screw up too.

LEE   No, you can't. You've got too many people depending on you. Like Mom and Arlene.

OWEN   (*moving away, right*) No.

LEE   Owen, I expect you to be there when they need you. So, you'd better grow up real fast.

OWEN	No! I can't even get my own life straight. How do you expect me to help somebody else? It should be me dying, Lee. Not you. They're leaving the wrong person in charge here. I mean, look at how I messed up this weekend alone.
LEE	Oh, for Christsake!
OWEN	No. No, you don't want someone like me looking out for your kids. Forget it.
LEE	No, I won't forget it. And who the hell do you think you are telling me I should've let you grow up on your own? You make it sound as if this whole mess is my fault.
OWEN	Well, you're the one who's dying, not me.
LEE	Yeah, well, believe me, Owen, I'm real sorry about that. And I'm sorry I spent most of my life trying to keep you out of trouble. I'm sorry I let you quit school after Dad died, and I'm sorry I got you that goddamn job at the plant!
OWEN	I got that job myself.
LEE	No, *I* got you that job. I got it! I practically had to beg Harvey to hire you on. The only reason you're working there right now is because you're Dad's son and my brother. And you think you're moving up? Huh? Well, I've got news for you. Harvey's not going to make you foreman. Not now. Not after I'm gone. Not ever! And I don't blame him. You haven't earned it. The truth is, you only wanted to work there in the first place because you thought it was safe. Because you thought they'd never fire one of the Melville boys. No. Our family's been there too long for that.
OWEN	I went to work there because I thought it was expected of me.
LEE	Expected of you? By who? By Dad? He didn't want you working there. You were his last hope. The last

one in the family who had a chance to be something. I missed my chance. Dad knew that. And he didn't want the same thing to happen to you.

OWEN   That's a lie.

LEE   It's the truth.

OWEN   Then why did you get me the job? If you knew all this, why'd you get me the job in the first place?

LEE   (*pause*) I was jealous. I didn't want you to do better than me. I didn't want you to have that chance. I mean, I saw myself trying to raise a family, and take care of Mom, and keep an eye on you. I didn't have any control over where my life was going. And then, there you were, like you've always been... like you didn't have a care in the world. There were times, Owen, when I couldn't even look at you without wanting to beat the hell out of you. And then, when I got you the job, I thought, "Well, now he's finally going to see what it's like. Now, he's finally going to see." (*beat*) I didn't know you were going to wind up liking the job, you stupid son of a bitch.

OWEN   So, what do you want from me now, Lee? Huh? You want me to pick up where you left off? With no control? With a family I didn't ask for?

LEE   All I want is for you to help. I just want to know you're going to help them. Don't you understand? The only thing I have to show for my thirty-three years is my family. And if I leave now, without making sure they're going to be looked after, then I've failed them too.

OWEN   No, you're not going to do this to me, Lee! You're not going to put this on me.

LEE   I'm not asking you to move in with them. I just want you to tell me that if they do need you, you'll be there. Just tell me that.

OWEN   I'm gonna get packed. (*moves to the bedroom, right*)

LEE   Owen, I need an answer... Owen?!

OWEN   (*stopping at the bedroom door; he doesn't look back*)
             I can't give you one, Lee... I can't. I'm sorry. (*exits
             to the bedroom*)

LEE   (*desperate*) Owen, please... Owen? (*moves slowly to the
             table, then in a fit of rage knocks the beer cans on to the
             floor*) Goddamn you!!

             *After a few seconds, OWEN enters from the bedroom.
             He stalks LEE.*

OWEN   I don't care what you say, and I don't care what
             Harvey says. I am gonna be the next foreman there,
             goddamn it. That job is gonna be mine!

             LEE goes about picking up the beer cans.

             And you can call me a stupid son of a bitch all you
             want, but the fact is, I do like working there. Yeah.
             And you know why? It's because... because, when I
             go in there every day, I know that there's gonna be
             no one in there who thinks they're better than me.
             No one! And if I go back to school and get a job
             somewhere else, then I can't be sure it's gonna be
             like that, can I? No. No, you're the one who
             should've done better for himself, Lee. Not me. I
             belong in that plant, and I'm gonna stay in there.
             And I'll tell you something else. And I mean this as
             a warning. If those kids of yours.... If those kids give
             me a hard time, they're gonna find out who's boss,
             and I mean in one helluva hurry. You make sure they
             know that. I'm not gonna take any crap. They do
             what I tell them to the first time, or else! (*turns away
             from LEE, and moans*) Two little girls. Why couldn't
             you have boys? I could take boys to a ball game.
             Teach them how to bunt. I ain't seen a girl yet who
             knew how to lay down a good bunt. And I'm not
             gonna be running errands for Arlene all the time
             either. She's a big girl. She can do these things for
             herself. I'm not an errand boy. You tell her that!

LEE   I will.

OWEN   All right. Are we settled?

LEE   (*quietly*) Yeah, we're settled.

OWEN   Good. (*looks around the room*) Boy, this is one helluva mess you got here. Aunt Rose is going to hang you out to dry.

LEE   It won't take long to clean up.

OWEN   Yeah, I suppose. (*beat*) Well, while you're doing that, I'm going to finally get some fishing done. (*moves to pick up his rod and tackle box*)

LEE   Owen?

OWEN   Yeah?

LEE   Uh... thanks for... you know. (*close to tears*)

OWEN   Hey, don't thank me until we find out how the girls turn out. I mean, I'm not "Father Knows Best."

OWEN starts to leave, then turns back.

OWEN   Oh, by the way, Mary said to say good-bye to you.

LEE   Mary?

OWEN   Yeah. She said she had a good time last night. And, she said to tell you she was going to buy a new car.

LEE   (*smiling*) Well, good for her. (*leans his hand on the counter*)

OWEN   Oh, and she left you a present. (*points to the cake, which is sitting on the counter near LEE's hand*)

LEE   Huh?

LEE looks down beside his hand where OWEN is pointing. He leaps back as if the cake is some sort of poisonous spider.

LEE   Oh! (*moves downstage centre away from the cake*)

OWEN   (*moving to LEE*) Hey, Lee, tell me something. Didn't you even want to go to bed with Mary?

LEE   What? What's that got to do with anything?

OWEN   Aw, come on, tell me. I gotta know.

LEE   Well... sure I did. Hey, I'm dying. I'm not crazy.

OWEN   (*with relief*) I knew it. Oh, thank God. Now I don't feel so stupid. You know what I did this morning?

LEE   What?

OWEN   Well, I sort of asked Loretta to marry me.

LEE   (*after a few seconds of staring to gather it in*) You did what?

OWEN   Yeah. And guess what she said.

LEE   You're out of your goddamn mind!

OWEN   (*beat*) That's a helluva guess. (*laughs, and exits*)

> *LEE moves upstage to the kitchen area, breaks an egg into the bowl, and starts mixing.*

(*offstage left*) Hey, hi there!!

> *LEE freezes. There are about two or three seconds silence.*

Hey girls, come on up!!

LEE   Owen? (*puts the bowl down and rushes out the screen door, left*) Owen!!! (*exits*)

> *Lights down.*

> *The end.*

OTHER TITLES
BY NORM FOSTER

THE AFFECTIONS OF MAY

DRINKING ALONE

ETHAN CLAYMORE

THE FOURSOME

HERE ON THE FLIGHT PATH

JUPITER IN JULY

THE LAST RESORT

THE LONG WEEKEND

MAGGIE'S GETTING MARRIED

THE MOTOR TRADE

NED DURANGO COMES TO BIG OAK

OFFICE HOURS

OPENING NIGHT

SINNERS

SMALL TIME

WRONG FOR EACH OTHER

Available from Playwrights Union of Canada
416-703-0201   fax 703-0059
orders@puc.ca   http://www.puc.ca